TEASPOON

THE AUSTRALIAN Women's Weekly

Stews, casseroles and curries

TRIPLE TESTED

THE AUSTRALIAN WOMEN'S WEEKLY TEST KITCHEN

PUBLISHED IN 2018 BY BAUER MEDIA BOOKS, AUSTRALIA.
BAUER MEDIA BOOKS IS A DIVISION OF BAUER MEDIA PTY LTD.

Bauer Media Books

Publisher Jo Runciman
Editorial & food director Sophia Young
Director of sales, marketing & rights Brian Cearnes
Editorial director-at-large Pamela Clark
Creative director Hannah Blackmore
Cover designer Jeannel Cunanan
Designer Gayna Murphy
Managing editor Stephanie Kistner
Junior editor Amanda Lees
Operations manager David Scotto

Cover photographer James Moffatt
Cover stylist Kate Brown
Cover photochefs Amal Webster, Angela Devlin

Printed in China
by Leo Paper Products Ltd.

A catalogue record for this book is available from the National Library of Australia.
ISBN: 978-1-74245-990-5 (paperback)

Published by Bauer Media Books,
a division of Bauer Media Pty Ltd,
54 Park St, Sydney; GPO Box 4088,
Sydney, NSW 2001, Australia
Ph +61 2 9282 8618; Fax +61 2 9126 3702
www.awwcookbooks.com.au

Order books
phone 136 116 (within Australia)
or order online at
www.awwcookbooks.com.au
Send recipe enquiries to
recipeenquiries@bauer-media.com.au

THE AUSTRALIAN
Women's Weekly

Stews, casseroles and curries

IRISH METAL
INDUSTRIES LTD

Contents

BEEF, LAMB & PORK

PREP + COOK TIME 3 HOURS 30 MINUTES   SERVES 6

LAMB SHANKS
with mash & silver beet

Lamb shanks are the perfect slow-cooked meat, due to their high level of collagen, which when cooked low and slow over a significant period of time, causes the meat to fall lusciously from the bone and become a soft, melt-in-your mouth texture.

¼ cup (60ml) olive oil
6 french-trimmed lamb shanks (1.2kg)
5 cloves garlic, peeled
1 large onion (200g), chopped coarsely
2 tablespoons tomato paste
1½ cups (375ml) dry red wine
2 cups (500ml) beef stock
400g (12½ ounces) canned diced tomatoes
1 tablespoon white (granulated) sugar
4 sprigs fresh rosemary
1kg (2 pounds) silver beet (swiss chard), stalks trimmed

mash

1.4kg (2¾ pounds) floury potatoes (see tips), peeled, halved
100g (3 ounces) butter, chopped
½ cup (125ml) thickened (heavy) cream, warmed

1 Preheat oven to 150°C/300°F.
2 Heat 1 tablespoon of the oil in a large flameproof casserole dish over medium-high heat; cook lamb, in two batches, for 5 minutes or until browned all over. Remove from dish.
3 Crush 3 garlic cloves; add crushed garlic and onion to same dish; cook, stirring, for 3 minutes or until onion softens. Add paste; cook, stirring, for 2 minutes. Stir in wine, bring to the boil; boil for 5 minutes or until reduced by half.
4 Return lamb to dish; add stock, tomatoes, sugar and rosemary. Transfer to oven; cook, covered, for 2 hours. Remove lid; cook for a further 1 hour or until lamb is tender.
5 Meanwhile, make mash.
6 Thinly slice remaining garlic. Heat remaining oil in a large frying pan on medium heat, add sliced garlic; cook, stirring, for 1 minute. Add silver beet; cook, stirring, for 3 minutes or until wilted.
7 Serve shanks with mash and silver beet, drizzled with cooking liquid.

mash Place potato in a large saucepan of cold salted water. Cover; bring to the boil. Cook until tender. Drain, return to pan over low heat; cook for 1 minute or until excess moisture has evaporated. Mash with butter and cream until smooth. Season to taste.

TIPS Floury potatoes have a high starch content so tend to fall apart when cooked. They are great for roasting, as their flesh becomes fluffy and the outside crisp, and for mashing. This recipe is suitable to freeze for up to 3 months at the end of step 4.

PREP + COOK TIME 1 HOUR 10 MINUTES SERVES 4

CHILLI BEEF
with cornbread dumplings

Cornbread is a quintessential Southern American staple, here served as dumplings with the equally recognisable bean and beef chilli. This is a great one-pot dinner and perfect for a weeknight family dinner. Omit the cayenne pepper if you don't like it spicy.

1 tablespoon olive oil
1 medium brown onion (150g), chopped coarsely
800g (1½ pounds) minced (ground) beef
3 cloves garlic, crushed
2 teaspoons ground cumin
2 teaspoons smoked paprika
½ teaspoon cayenne pepper
400g (12½ ounces) canned kidney beans, drained, rinsed
800g (1½ pounds) canned diced tomatoes
1 cup (250ml) beef stock
1 cup (250ml) water
1 tablespoon brown sugar

cornbread dumplings

1⅓ cups (200g) self-raising flour
⅓ cup (55g) polenta
¼ cup (30g) coarsely grated cheddar
¼ cup (60g) creamed corn
1 egg, beaten lightly
½ cup (125ml) milk

1 Heat oil in a large saucepan; cook onion, beef, garlic and spices, stirring, until beef is browned.

2 Add beans to pan with tomatoes, stock, the water and sugar; bring to the boil. Reduce heat; simmer, for 30 minutes, stirring occasionally. Season to taste.

3 Meanwhile, make cornbread dumplings.

4 Roll level tablespoons of the dumpling mixture into balls and place on top of beef mixture in pan; cook, covered, for 15 minutes or until dumplings are cooked.

cornbread dumplings Combine sifted flour, polenta and cheddar in a medium bowl; stir in corn, egg and milk.

TIPS Use wet hands when rolling the dumplings to stop them sticking. Use a wide saucepan so you have more surface area for the dumplings to cook.

PREP + COOK TIME 1 HOUR 50 MINUTES (+ STANDING) SERVES 4

BEEF & PORCINI MUSHROOM STEW *with parmesan mash*

Mushrooms have a moreish savoury taste known as 'umami', and are a good source of vitamins B and D. Here they add a richness to the stew along with the beef, accompanied with the cheesy parmesan mash so that none of the delicious juices are wasted.

25g (¾ ounce) dried porcini mushrooms
1 cup (250ml) beef stock
2 tablespoons olive oil
1.5kg (3 pounds) gravy beef, cut into 5cm (2-inch) pieces
1 large onion (200g), chopped coarsely
2 cloves garlic, crushed
2 tablespoons tomato paste
400g (12½ ounces) canned cherry tomatoes
1 bay leaf
250g (4 ounces) button mushrooms, halved
2 tablespoons coarsely chopped fresh flat-leaf parsley

parmesan mash

1kg (2 pounds) floury potatoes (see tips), peeled, cut into large pieces
¾ cup (180ml) pouring cream
75g (2½ ounces) butter, chopped
1 cup (80g) finely grated parmesan

1 Place porcini mushrooms and stock in a small bowl; stand for 10 minutes. Drain, reserving stock. Finely chop mushrooms.

2 Heat oil in a large flameproof casserole dish or heavy-based saucepan over medium-high heat; cook beef, in batches, turning until browned all over. Remove from dish.

3 Cook onion and garlic in same dish, stirring, for 3 minutes or until softened. Return beef to dish; add paste, tomatoes, bay leaf, porcini mushrooms and reserved stock. Bring to the boil, reduce heat to low; simmer, covered, for 30 minutes. Add button mushrooms; cook, uncovered, for a further 1 hour or until meat is tender. Season to taste.

4 Meanwhile, make parmesan mash.

5 Serve stew with parmesan mash, sprinkled with parsley.

parmesan mash Boil potato in a saucepan of salted water for 15 minutes or until tender. Drain; leave for a few minutes to dry. Heat cream and butter in same pan over low-medium heat; add potato, mashing into milk mixture with a potato masher until smooth. Remove from heat; stir in parmesan until combined. Season to taste.

TIPS Floury potatoes have a high starch content so tend to fall apart when cooked. They are great for roasting, as their flesh becomes fluffy and the outside crisp, and for mashing. If you use a potato ricer to mash potatoes, add pressed potatoes to the warm cream, then stir the butter and parmesan in.

PREP + COOK TIME 4 HOURS 15 MINUTES SERVES 6

SLOW-BRAISED BEEF
with torn pasta & lemon pangrattato

Here we have served the slow-braised beef with fresh sheets of lasagne, torn into long pieces to serve as larger than average pasta strands. You can use any fresh pasta of your choice instead of the lasagne sheets, or large pasta shells, if you prefer.

2 tablespoons olive oil
1.5kg (3-pound) piece beef chuck
2 cups (500ml) beef stock
¾ cup (180ml) sweet sherry
1 tablespoon finely chopped preserved lemon rind
50g (1½ ounces) butter
6 cloves garlic, sliced thinly
400g (12½ ounces) fresh lasagne pasta sheets, torn into pieces
1 small red onion (100g), halved, sliced thinly

lemon pangrattato

25g (¾ ounce) butter
2 cups (200g) coarse fresh breadcrumbs (see tips)
2 cloves garlic, sliced
¼ cup chopped mixed soft herbs (flat-leaf parsley, mint, coriander)
2 teaspoons finely chopped preserved lemon rind

1 Preheat oven to 160°C/325°C.
2 Heat oil in a flameproof casserole dish over medium-high heat; cook beef for 5 minutes or until browned all over. Add stock, sherry, preserved lemon rind, butter and garlic. Transfer to oven; cook, covered, for 3¾ hours or until meat falls apart. Remove beef from dish; pull apart into large pieces.
3 Meanwhile, make lemon pangrattato.
4 Skim fat from surface of cooking liquid in dish. Place dish on stove over low heat; cook for 15 minutes or until liquid has thickened and reduced by half. Return beef pieces to dish. Season to taste.
5 Cook pasta in a large saucepan of boiling salted water for 2 minutes or until just tender; drain.
6 Add pasta and red onion to beef mixture; toss to mix well. Serve topped with pangrattato.

lemon pangrattato Combine butter, breadcrumbs and garlic in a medium bowl; season. Spread mixture on an oven tray; bake in oven for the last 15 minutes of beef cooking time or until golden. Stir in herbs and preserved lemon rind.

TIPS To make 2 cups fresh breadcrumbs, process 4 slices of stale bread until coarse crumbs form. This braised beef would also be great in lasagne or soup or to fill a pie or tacos.

PREP + COOK TIME 45 MINUTES SERVES 4

SMOKED PORK SAUSAGE & kipfler goulash

Originally a stew from Hungary, a goulash is characterised by its spices, particularly smoked paprika, and is known for its hearty nature. Here we use pork sausage meat and kipfler potatoes to cut down cooking time and have dinner on the table in no time at all.

2 tablespoons olive oil
500g (1 pound) good-quality pork sausages
2 small red onions (200g), cut into wedges
500g (1 pound) small kipfler (fingerling) potatoes, scrubbed, halved lengthways
2 cloves garlic, crushed
2 tablespoons tomato paste
2¼ teaspoons smoked paprika
½ teaspoon fennel seeds
400g (12½ ounces) canned crushed tomatoes
1 cup (250ml) chicken stock
⅓ cup (80g) sour cream
½ cup (55g) coarsely chopped walnuts, toasted
baby parsley leaves, to serve

1 Heat oil in a large heavy-based frying pan over high heat. Squeeze pieces of sausage out of skins into pan; cook, stirring occasionally, for 5 minutes or until golden brown. Remove from pan with a slotted spoon; drain on paper towel.
2 Add onion and potato to same pan; cook, stirring occasionally, for 5 minutes or until onion softens. Return sausage to pan, add garlic, paste, 2 teaspoons of the paprika and fennel seeds; cook, stirring, for 2 minutes or until fragrant. Add tomatoes and stock; bring to the boil. Reduce heat to medium; simmer, covered, for 20 minutes or until potato is tender and sauce reduces slightly. Season.
3 Serve goulash topped with sour cream, walnuts, remaining paprika and parsley.

TIPS Goulash can be made up until the end of step 2 up to 2 days ahead and stored in an airtight container in the fridge. Recipe is not suitable to freeze.

PREP + COOK TIME 3 HOURS SERVES 6

lamb shank tagine
WITH CAULIFLOWER COUSCOUS

A tagine is a Moroccan dish named after the earthenware pot it is cooked in, usually rich in spices and dotted with dried fruits. Instead of the traditional couscous, here we have paired the lamb with low-carb cauliflower that has been processed so that it resembles cooked grains.

1 tablespoon olive oil
6 french-trimmed lamb shanks (1.6kg)
2 medium onions (300g), chopped coarsely
3 cloves garlic, sliced thinly
2 fresh long red chillies, sliced thinly
1 medium red capsicum (bell pepper) (200g), chopped coarsely
2 cinnamon sticks
1 teaspoon ground ginger
1 teaspoon sweet paprika
2 teaspoons ground cumin
2 tablespoons tomato paste
400g (12½ ounces) canned chopped tomatoes
1½ cups (375ml) chicken stock
3 fresh dates, pitted, chopped finely
½ cup (140g) Greek-style yoghurt
¼ cup fresh flat-leaf parsley leaves

cauliflower couscous

1 small cauliflower (1kg), trimmed, cut into florets
2 tablespoons olive oil
2 tablespoons lemon juice
½ cup coarsely chopped fresh flat-leaf parsley

1 Preheat oven to 160°C/325°F.

2 Heat oil in a large flameproof casserole dish over medium-high heat; cook lamb for 2 minutes on each side or until browned. Remove from dish.

3 Cook onion, garlic, chilli, capsicum and cinnamon in same dish over medium heat, stirring, for 3 minutes or until onion softens. Add spices; cook, stirring, for 2 minutes or until fragrant. Stir in paste, tomatoes, stock and dates. Return lamb to dish; bring to the boil. Transfer to oven; cook, covered, for 2½ hours or until lamb is almost falling off the bone, turning halfway during cooking time. Season to taste.

4 Meanwhile, make cauliflower couscous.

5 Top lamb with yoghurt and parsley; season. Serve with cauliflower couscous.

cauliflower couscous Pulse cauliflower, in batches, into couscous-size pieces in a food processor. Heat oil in a large frying pan over medium-high heat; cook cauliflower, stirring, for 7 minutes or until cauliflower is tender and lightly browned. Stir in lemon juice and parsley. Season to taste.

TIP Tagine will keep, covered, in the fridge for up to 3 days.

PREP + COOK TIME 2 HOURS 50 MINUTES (+ COOLING) SERVES 6

PORK & FENNEL RAGÙ

with sweet potato gnocchi

- 1.6kg (3¼-pound) piece boneless pork shoulder
- 2 tablespoons plain (all-purpose) flour
- 1 tablespoon extra virgin olive oil
- 2 medium leeks (700g), white part only, sliced thinly
- 2 trimmed celery stalks (200g), chopped coarsely
- 2 medium fennel bulbs (600g), sliced thinly, fronds reserved
- 4 cloves garlic, chopped
- 1 teaspoon chopped fresh thyme leaves
- ¼ teaspoon dried chilli flakes
- 2 cups (500ml) chicken stock
- 2 cups (500ml) water
- 1 cup (120g) green sicilian olives
- 1 tablespoon lemon juice

sweet potato gnocchi

- 1kg (2 pounds) orange sweet potato, unpeeled
- 120g (4 ounces) soft goat's cheese, crumbled
- 2 egg yolks
- 1 cup (150g) plain (all-purpose) flour, approximately

1 Remove rind and trim fat from pork. Cut pork into six pieces, toss in flour; shake away excess. Heat oil in a flameproof casserole dish over high heat; cook pork, in batches, for 10 minutes or until browned lightly all over. Remove from dish.

2 Cook leek, celery and sliced fennel in same dish stirring, over medium heat for 8 minutes or until softened. Add garlic, thyme and chilli; cook, stirring, for 1 minute or until fragrant. Add stock and the water; bring to the boil. Return pork to dish; stir to cover with liquid. Reduce heat to low; cook, covered, stirring occasionally, for 2 hours or until tender.

3 Meanwhile, make sweet potato gnocchi.

4 Remove pork from pan; shred into smaller pieces. Return pork to pan; add olives and juice. Season to taste. Cover; keep warm over low heat.

5 Cook gnocchi, in batches, in a large saucepan of boiling salted water for 2 minutes or until gnocchi float to the surface. Remove gnocchi with a slotted spoon; drain on paper towel.

6 Top gnocchi with ragù; serve sprinkled with reserved fennel fronds and extra thyme leaves, if you like.

sweet potato gnocchi Place whole sweet potato in a medium saucepan, cover with cold water. Cover pan with lid; bring to the boil. Reduce heat to low-medium; simmer, partially covered, for 45 minutes or until tender. Drain. Cool slightly; peel. Mash sweet potato in a large bowl until smooth. Cool to room temperature. Stir in cheese and egg yolks; season. Add enough of the flour to form a soft, slightly sticky dough. Divide dough into six portions; roll each portion on a floured workbench into a 2cm (¾-inch) thick log. Using a floured knife, cut logs into 2cm (¾ inch) lengths. Place gnocchi, in a single layer, on a large plastic-wrap-lined tray. Cover; refrigerate until required.

TIPS Prepare the ragù several hours or a day ahead; refrigerate until cold then remove any fat from the surface before reheating. You can use drained persian fetta instead of goat's cheese, if you prefer.

Mashes

BASIC POTATO MASH

PREP + COOK TIME 30 minutes **SERVES** 4

Place 1kg (2lbs) peeled, coarsely chopped potatoes (see tip) in a medium saucepan with enough cold water to barely cover them. Boil, over medium heat, for 15 minutes or until potato is tender; drain. Return potato to pan, mash until smooth (or use a potato ricer or mouli). Add 40g (1½oz) butter and ¾ cup (180ml) hot milk; fold in gently until mash is smooth. Season to taste. Serve as is, or with one of the flavour variations, opposite.

TIP Floury and all-rounder potatoes are best for mash; try coliban, toolangi delight, king edward or dutch cream.

MUSTARD & CHEDDAR

Make Basic Potato Mash (left). When adding the butter and milk, also add 2 tablespoons dijon or wholegrain mustard and 1 cup grated vintage cheddar. Return pan to heat; stir mash over medium heat until smooth and cheese melts. Season to taste. Serve topped with extra grated vintage cheddar.

OLIVE OIL & SAGE

Boil 1kg (2lbs) potatoes as directed for Basic Potato Mash (left); drain. Wipe pan dry. Heat ⅓ cup olive oil in same pan; fry 2 thinly sliced cloves garlic and 2 tablespoons sage leaves until crisp. Remove with a slotted spoon. Return potatoes to pan with ½ cup hot milk; mash until smooth. Season to taste. Serve topped with garlic and sage.

KALE

Boil 1kg (2lbs) potatoes as directed for Basic Potato Mash (left); drain. Wipe pan dry. Heat ⅓ cup olive oil in pan; cook 125g (4oz) shredded kale and 1 chopped clove garlic, stirring, over medium heat for 5 minutes until kale wilts. Remove from pan. Return potatoes to pan with 30g (1oz) butter and ¾ cup hot milk; mash until smooth. Stir in kale; season to taste.

PREP + COOK TIME 3 HOURS 50 MINUTES SERVES 4

BRAISED BEEF CHEEKS
with minted carrot puree

Beef cheeks are an amazingly economical cut of beef, very tough if cooked normally, but tender and moreish when cooked long and slow. It absorbs any braising liquid and in turn pulls apart and falls to pieces when ready to be eaten.

⅓ cup (80ml) olive oil
4 beef cheeks (1.6kg), trimmed
1 medium onion (150g), chopped finely
1 medium carrot (120g), chopped finely
1 sprig fresh rosemary
1 tablespoon white spelt flour
1⅓ cups (330ml) dark beer
½ cup (125ml) dry red wine
¼ cup (70g) tomato paste
2 cups (500ml) beef stock
2 cups (500ml) water
¼ cup fresh mint leaves

minted carrot puree

3 sprigs fresh mint, leaves removed, stems reserved
3 large carrots (540g), sliced thinly
30g (1 ounce) butter, chopped
3 cups (750ml) water

1 Preheat oven to 150°C/300°F.

2 Heat half the oil in a large heavy-based saucepan over medium heat. Season beef; cook, turning, for 5 minutes or until browned all over. Remove from pan.

3 Heat remaining oil in same pan over medium heat. Add onion, carrot and rosemary; cook, stirring, for 10 minutes or until vegetables soften.

4 Add flour; cook, stirring, until mixture bubbles and thickens. Add beer, wine, paste, stock, the water and beef; bring to the boil. Reduce heat; simmer, covered, for 3½ hours or until beef is very tender and starting to fall apart; season.

5 Meanwhile, make minted carrot puree.

6 Serve carrot puree topped with beef cheeks, drizzled with pan juices and sprinkled with mint.

minted carrot puree Finely chop mint leaves; set aside. Place carrot, butter, the water and reserved mint stems in a medium saucepan; bring to the boil. Reduce heat to low; cook for 15 minutes or until carrots are tender. Discard stems. Drain, reserving cooking liquid. Blend or process carrot mixture with 2 tablespoons of the reserved cooking liquid, adding more cooking liquid if necessary, until smooth. Stir in chopped mint; season to taste.

serving suggestion Serve with braised greens, such as kale, cavolo nero, cabbage or spinach leaves.

PREP + COOK TIME 4 HOURS 30 MINUTES (+ REFRIGERATION) **SERVES** 6

stout beef RIBS

Stout and dark brown sugar provide the central flavours of the marinade for our finger-licking beef ribs. These rich ingredients pair perfectly together, contrasted with the spicy bite of the fresh chilli and create a perfect sauce when reduced to accompany the tender ribs.

1½ cups (375ml) dark stout
⅔ cup (150g) firmly packed dark brown sugar
¾ cup (180ml) apple cider vinegar
2 fresh small red chillies, chopped finely
¼ cup (70g) wholegrain mustard
2kg (4 pounds) piece beef short spare ribs

1 Combine stout, sugar, vinegar, chilli and mustard in a medium bowl; stir until sugar dissolves. Pour mixture over ribs in a glass or ceramic dish; toss to coat. Cover; refrigerate for 2 hours or overnight.
2 Preheat oven to 180°C/350°F.
3 Place ribs and marinade in a roasting pan; cover with foil. Roast for 3 hours. Remove foil; roast for a further 1 hour or until meat is tender and almost falling off the bone. Transfer ribs to a platter; cover to keep warm.
4 Place pan on stove top over low-medium heat; bring marinade mixture to a simmer. Simmer for 10 minutes or until thick and syrupy.
5 Slice ribs; serve with reduced sauce.

serving suggestion Serve with a watercress and baby fennel salad.

PREP + COOK TIME 3 HOURS (+ STANDING) SERVES 4

LAMB SHANK & bean ragù

You need to soak the dried beans for at least 8 hours before starting this recipe.

½ cup (100g) dried haricot beans
½ cup (100g) dried borlotti beans
2 tablespoons plain (all-purpose) flour
8 french-trimmed lamb shanks (1.6kg)
2 tablespoons olive oil
1 large onion (200g), chopped
1 medium carrot (120g), chopped
1 celery stalk (150g), trimmed, chopped coarsely
2 cloves garlic, crushed
1 fresh long red chilli, chopped finely
¼ cup (60ml) balsamic vinegar
400g (12½ ounces) canned crushed tomatoes
8 anchovies
1 cinnamon stick
2 sprigs fresh rosemary
½ cup (125ml) red wine
2 cups (500ml) water
⅓ cup fresh flat-leaf parsley sprigs

1 Place dried beans in a large bowl, cover with cold water; soak for 8 hours or overnight.
2 Drain soaked beans, rinse under cold water; drain. Place beans in a medium saucepan, cover with water; bring to the boil. Reduce heat to low; cook for 15 minutes (beans will not be fully cooked at this stage). Drain.
3 Preheat oven to 180°C/350°F.
4 Place flour in a medium bowl; season with salt and pepper. Toss lamb in flour; shake away excess. Heat half the oil in a large flameproof casserole dish over medium heat; cook lamb, in batches, turning, for 5 minutes or until browned all over. Remove from dish. Wipe dish clean if necessary.
5 Heat remaining oil in dish over medium heat; cook onion, carrot, celery, garlic and chilli, stirring, for 5 minutes or until vegetables soften.
6 Return lamb to dish, add beans, vinegar, tomatoes, anchovies, cinnamon, rosemary, wine and the water; bring to the boil. Transfer to oven; cook, covered, for 1 hour, turning shanks halfway through cooking. Uncover; cook for a further 1 hour or until meat is almost falling off the bone.
7 Just before serving, stir parsley through ragù.

serving suggestion Serve ragù with polenta or creamy mashed potato.

PREP + COOK TIME 3 HOURS SERVES 4

CIDER-BRAISED PORK
with pancetta lentils & apples

French-style green lentils are related to the famous French lentils du puy; these green-blue, tiny lentils have a hardy nature that allows them to be rapidly cooked without disintegrating. You can also serve the lentils with grilled sausages, pan-fried salmon or roast chicken.

1.5kg (3 pounds) boneless pork neck (scotch fillet)
⅓ cup (80ml) olive oil
1 medium leek (350g), white part only, sliced thinly
2 teaspoons fennel seeds, crushed lightly
2 teaspoons coriander seeds, crushed lightly
2⅔ cups (660ml) apple cider
100g (3 ounces) pancetta, chopped finely
1 small onion (80g), chopped finely
1 small carrot (70g), chopped finely
1 celery stalk (150g), trimmed, chopped finely
1 clove garlic, crushed
¼ cup (60ml) dry white wine
1 bay leaf
2 sprigs fresh thyme
2 cups (500ml) chicken stock
1½ cups (375ml) water
1 cup (200g) dried French-style green lentils, rinsed
4 medium fresh apples (600g), quartered

1 Preheat oven to 160°C/325°F.
2 Trim excess fat from pork. Tie pork with kitchen string at 3cm (1¼-inch) intervals.
3 Heat 2 tablespoons of the oil in a large flameproof casserole dish over medium-high heat; cook pork, turning, for 8 minutes or until browned all over. Remove pork from dish.
4 Add leek to dish, reduce heat to low; cook, stirring, for 5 minutes or until softened. Add seeds; cook, stirring, for 1 minute or until fragrant. Return pork to dish; add cider and bring to the boil. Transfer to oven; cook, covered, for 2 hours. Remove lid; turn pork, cook for a further 30 minutes or until pork is very tender.
5 Meanwhile, for braised lentils, heat 1 tablespoon oil in a large frying pan over medium heat. Add pancetta, onion, carrot, celery and garlic; cook, stirring occasionally, for 7 minutes or until vegetables soften. Increase heat to medium-high, add wine, bay leaf and thyme; cook for 1 minute or until most of the cooking liquid evaporates. Add stock, the water and lentils; bring to the boil. Reduce heat; simmer, partially covered, for 20 minutes or until lentils are tender. Discard bay leaf and thyme sprigs. Season to taste.
6 Heat remaining oil in a large frying pan over high heat. Add apple and ¾ cup (180ml) of the pork braising liquid, bring to the boil, cook, turning apples halfway during cooking, for 5 minutes or until apples are coloured and heated through and braising liquid reduces by half; season to taste.
7 Serve pork with apple, any pan juices and with pancetta lentils.

PREP + COOK TIME 45 MINUTES SERVES 4

VEAL, MUSHROOMS & POTATOES *with cream sauce*

This simple dish is packed with warming and comforting flavours, crème fraîche adding a fresh, tangy note to the traditional cream sauce. Serve this one-pan meal with a crisp garden salad, if you like.

60g (2 ounces) butter
400g (12½ ounces) veal fillet, sliced thinly
3 shallots (75g), halved
200g (6½ ounces) swiss brown mushrooms, sliced
500g (1 pound) kipfler (fingerling) potatoes, cut into 1cm (½-inch) rounds
⅓ cup (80ml) dry white wine
1 cup (250ml) chicken stock
1 tablespoon worcestershire sauce
2 teaspoons dijon mustard
250g (8 ounces) crème fraîche
¼ cup chopped fresh chives
50g (1½ ounces) baby spinach leaves

1 Melt a third of the butter in a large non-stick frying pan over high heat; cook veal for 1 minute on each side or until browned lightly. Transfer to a plate; cover to keep warm.

2 Heat another third of the butter in same pan, add shallots and mushrooms; cook, stirring, for 5 minutes or until liquid has evaporated. Remove from pan.

3 Melt remaining butter in same pan, add potato; cook, stirring, for 10 minutes or until lightly browned and tender. Remove from the pan.

4 Add wine to pan, cook, stirring, for 1 minute or until reduced slightly. Add stock, sauce and mustard; bring to the boil. Reduce heat to low-medium; simmer for 3 minutes or until reduced by half. Whisk in crème fraîche and half the chives.

5 Return potato, mushroom and veal to pan to warm through. Add spinach; stir to combine. Serve topped with remaining chives. Season to taste.

TIPS Swiss brown mushrooms have a stronger flavour than button mushrooms, which can be used instead, if you prefer. Recipe is not suitable to freeze.

PREP + COOK TIME 1 HOUR SERVES 4

MEATBALL TAGINE
with baked eggs

Baked eggs are a delicious breakfast food, and here we adapt them to be a filling protein-rich dinner with the inclusion of the spiced meatballs. Serve this tagine with Greek-style yoghurt and grilled pitta bread to soak up the sauce.

500g (1 pound) minced (ground) beef
1 clove garlic, crushed
¼ cup finely chopped fresh mint
2 tablespoons finely chopped fresh coriander (cilantro)
1 teaspoon ground cinnamon
1 teaspoon ground coriander
2 teaspoons ground cumin
½ teaspoon chilli powder
1 tablespoon olive oil
1 medium onion (150g), chopped finely
4 large tomatoes (880g), chopped coarsely
pinch saffron threads
4 eggs
½ cup fresh coriander (cilantro) leaves

1 Combine beef, garlic, mint, chopped coriander, cinnamon, ground coriander, half the cumin and half the chilli in a large bowl; season. Roll level tablespoons of mixture into balls.

2 Heat oil in a tagine (see tip) or large heavy-based frying pan over medium heat; cook meatballs, in two batches, turning, for 5 minutes or until browned. Remove from tagine.

3 Cook onion in tagine, stirring, for 3 minutes or until softened. Add tomato, saffron and remaining cumin and chilli; bring to the boil. Reduce heat to low; cook for 15 minutes or until tomatoes soften.

4 Return meatballs to tagine; cook for 10 minutes or until meatballs are cooked through and sauce thickens slightly. Season to taste. Make four indents in the sauce; carefully crack eggs into indents; cook, covered, for 5 minutes or until whites of eggs are set and yolks remain runny (or eggs are cooked to your liking). Sprinkle tagine with coriander leaves.

TIP A tagine is both the name of the dish and the traditional vessel which is used for cooking it in. It has a flat-bottomed base and a conical lid, designed to trap the steam and keep the food moist. An enamelled cast-iron pan which holds the heat evenly is a good alternative.

PREP + COOK TIME 2 HOURS SERVES 4

Chinese-style STICKY LAMB RIBS

It's almost mandatory to eat ribs with your hands, and with this sticky sauce, rich with Chinese flavours, you'll be licking your fingers to get every last bit. Try and find young ginger for this recipe, as older ginger skin can be a little bitter.

1 tablespoon olive oil
1.5kg (3 pounds) lamb riblets
1 medium orange (240g), halved crossways
55g (2-ounce) piece fresh young ginger, unpeeled, sliced
6 cloves garlic, unpeeled, bruised
3 shallots (75g), unpeeled, halved
2 fresh long red chillies, chopped coarsely
2 cinnamon sticks, broken in half
3 whole star anise, cracked
½ cup (125ml) chinese cooking wine (shao hsing)
½ cup (125ml) salt-reduced soy sauce
⅓ cup (120g) honey
1 cup (250ml) beef stock
1 cup (250ml) water
1 bunch gai lan (200g)
½ cup (75g) roasted unsalted cashews, chopped coarsely

1 Heat oil in a large flameproof casserole dish over medium-high heat. Cook ribs, in batches, for 4 minutes or until browned.

2 Pour off any excess fat from dish (see tips). Return ribs to dish, add orange, ginger, garlic, shallots, chilli, cinnamon, star anise, cooking wine, soy sauce, honey, stock and the water; bring to the boil. Reduce heat to low; cook, covered, turning once halfway through, for 1½ hours or until ribs are tender.

3 Remove ribs from dish; cover to keep warm. Strain solids from liquid; discard. Return liquid to same dish; place over high heat. Boil for 20 minutes or until dark and sticky. Return ribs to dish, stir to coat in sauce and heat through.

4 Meanwhile, boil, steam or microwave gai lan until tender; drain.

5 Top ribs with cashews; serve with gai lan.

TIPS Rendered lamb fat can be strained through a fine metal sieve into a heatproof container and refrigerated for up to 3 months for use in cooking later. Gai lan is available from Asian food stores and major supermarkets; you can use any asian green you like.

PREP + COOK TIME 2 HOURS 30 MINUTES (+ STANDING) SERVES 6

BRAISED PORK NECK
& shiitake mushrooms

Like other secondary cuts of meat, pork neck is best cooked slow, as the long cooking time helps break down the intramuscular fat, keeping the meat moist and tender.

16 dried shiitake mushrooms (30g)
1.5kg (3-pound) piece pork neck (scotch fillet roast), fat trimmed
2 tablespoons dark soy sauce
2 tablespoons light soy sauce
5cm (2-inch) piece fresh ginger (25g), chopped coarsely
2 cloves garlic, chopped
1 stalk fresh lemon grass, chopped coarsely
4 kaffir lime leaves
2 tablespoons brown sugar
2 whole star anise
1 litre (4 cups) chicken stock
500g (1 pound) fresh rice noodles
1 cup fresh coriander (cilantro) leaves

1 Place mushrooms in a small bowl; cover with warm water. Stand for 30 minutes.
2 Place pork, soy sauces, ginger, garlic, lemon grass, lime leaves, sugar, star anise, drained mushrooms and stock in a heavy-based saucepan just large enough to hold the pork. Bring to the boil. Reduce heat to low; cook, covered, for 2 hours, turning occasionally (liquid won't cover pork completely).
3 Just before serving, cook noodles in a large saucepan of simmering water for 2 minutes; drain.
4 Transfer pork to a plate; cover, stand for 5 minutes. Discard star anise.
5 Slice pork; serve noodles topped with pork, mushrooms and coriander, drizzled with some of the cooking liquid.

serving suggestion Serve with steamed asian greens such as buk choy, choy sum or gai lan.

PREP + COOK TIME 2 HOURS SERVES 6

slow-cooked BOLOGNESE

Spaghetti bolognese is an Australian favourite, and a dinner classic that satisfies both adults and children alike. Our slow-cooked sauce takes the original and gives it a depth of flavour that only comes with hours reducing on the stove.

1 tablespoon olive oil
1 large onion (200g), chopped finely
2 celery stalks (300g), trimmed, chopped
2 large carrots (360g), chopped
100g (3 ounces) prosciutto, chopped finely
2 cloves garlic, crushed
1kg (2 pounds) minced (ground) pork and veal (see tips)
¼ cup (70g) tomato paste
1 teaspoon dried oregano leaves
1 cup (250ml) dry red wine
700g (1½ pounds) tomato passata
2 cups (500ml) beef stock
1 tablespoon chopped fresh rosemary leaves
2 sprigs fresh thyme
100g (3-ounce) block parmesan, rind removed and reserved
400g (12½ ounces) spaghetti

1 Heat oil in a large heavy-based saucepan over high heat; cook onion, celery, carrot, prosciutto and garlic, stirring, for 5 minutes or until onion is soft. Add pork and veal; cook, stirring, to break up lumps, for 10 minutes or until browned.

2 Stir in paste and oregano; cook, stirring, for 2 minutes. Add wine, bring to the boil; cook for 4 minutes or until reduced by half. Stir in passata, stock, rosemary, thyme and parmesan rind; bring to the boil. Reduce heat to low; cook, covered, stirring occasionally, for 1½ hours or until thickened. Season. Remove and discard parmesan rind from sauce.

3 Cook spaghetti in a large saucepan of boiling salted water for 8 minutes or until just tender; drain.

4 Finely grate remaining parmesan. Serve spaghetti topped with bolognese sauce, sprinkled with grated parmesan and fresh oregano leaves, if you like.

TIPS Use minced beef or a combination of minced beef and pork and veal, if you prefer. This recipe is suitable to freeze at the end of step 2.

PREP + COOK TIME 2 HOURS 20 MINUTES SERVES 4

IRISH STEW WITH *carrot-top salsa verde*

Using every part of the vegetable is a positive, for both your wallet and for the environment. By using the carrot tops in our salsa verde recipe we not only stop them ending up in the bin, but it also adds a nice fresh element to top off this meaty Irish stew.

⅓ cup (80ml) olive oil
1kg (2 pounds) boned lamb neck, cut into 5cm (2-inch) pieces
1 medium onion (150g), chopped
1 trimmed celery stalk (100g), chopped finely
3 cloves garlic, crushed
1.25 litres (5 cups) chicken stock
400g (12½ ounces) baby (dutch) carrots with tops, trimmed, tops reserved
1 medium swede (225g), cut into six wedges
½ cup (70g) roasted hazelnuts, chopped coarsely

carrot-top salsa verde

1½ cups loosely packed fresh flat-leaf parsley leaves
1½ tablespoons fresh lemon thyme leaves
1 tablespoon drained capers
1 small clove garlic, crushed
1 teaspoon brown sugar
½ cup (125ml) extra virgin olive oil
1½ tablespoons white wine vinegar

1 Heat 2 tablespoons of the oil in a large heavy-based saucepan over high heat; cook lamb, in batches, for 5 minutes, turning occasionally, until browned all over. Remove from pan. (If the base of the pan starts to burn, add 2 tablespoons water and stir to lift meat sticking to base of the pan.)

2 Reduce heat to medium, add remaining oil to pan; cook onion, celery and garlic, stirring occasionally, for 10 minutes or until softened. Return lamb to pan, add stock; bring to the boil. Reduce heat to low; cook, covered, for 2 hours or until meat is tender.

3 Meanwhile, wash reserved carrot tops; you need ½ cup firmly packed tops for salsa verde, and some extra to serve.

4 Make carrot-top salsa verde.

5 Increase pan heat to high; return to the boil. Add carrots and swede; simmer, uncovered, for 15 minutes or until liquid has thickened slightly. Season. Serve stew topped with hazelnuts and salsa verde.

carrot-top salsa verde Blend or process ingredients with reserved ½ cup carrot tops (from step 3) until well combined; season to taste. Refrigerate until needed.

TIP Storing baby carrots with the leaves attached reduces their keeping time dramatically. Cut the tops off as soon as you can. Wrap the tops in damp paper towel; refrigerate until needed.

Rices

STEAMED GINGER RICE

PREP + COOK TIME 20 MINUTES SERVES 4

Heat 1 tablespoon olive oil in a medium heavy-based saucepan; cook 6 thinly sliced green onions (scallions), stirring, until softened. Add 2½ teaspoons finely grated fresh ginger and 1½ cups basmati rice; stir to coat in oil. Add 2 cups chicken stock; bring to the boil. Reduce heat; simmer, covered, over low heat, 10 minutes. Remove from heat; stand, covered, 5 minutes, then fluff with fork. Stir in 2 tablespoons finely chopped fresh mint; season to taste.

COCONUT RICE

PREP + COOK TIME 20 MINUTES SERVES 4

Place 1½ cups (300g) jasmine rice, 270ml canned coconut milk, ⅔ cup water and 2 teaspoons finely grated fresh ginger in a heavy-based saucepan, season with salt; stir well to combine. Cover pan with a lid; bring to the boil over medium heat. Reduce heat to low; cook for 10 minutes. Turn off heat; stand, covered, for a further 5 minutes before removing lid.

CAULIFLOWER 'RICE' PILAF

PREP + COOK TIME 20 MINUTES SERVES 4

Process 1 coarsely chopped medium (1kg) cauliflower, in batches, until finely chopped. Heat 2 tablespoons olive oil in a large heavy-based frying pan over high heat. Add 1 teaspoon cumin seeds and cauliflower to frying pan; cook, stirring occasionally, for 12 minutes or until cauliflower is just tender. Stir in ¼ cup coarsely chopped fresh coriander (cilantro); season to taste.

BASMATI PILAF

PREP + COOK TIME 30 MINUTES SERVES 4

Melt 20g (¾oz) butter in a medium saucepan; cook 1 crushed garlic clove, stirring, until fragrant. Add 1 cup brown basmati rice; cook, stirring, 1 minute. Add 1 cup chicken stock and 1 cup water; bring to the boil. Reduce heat to low; simmer, covered, for 20 minutes or until rice is just tender. Remove from heat; fluff rice with fork. Stir in ¼ cup coarsely chopped fresh flat-leaf parsley and ¼ cup toasted flaked almonds.

PREP + COOK TIME 1 HOUR 30 MINUTES (+ STANDING) SERVES 4

SMOKY HAM & maple baked beans

You will need to start this recipe a day ahead.

2 cups (400g) dried cannellini beans
2 small onions (160g)
4 cloves garlic
6 x 10cm (4-inch) fresh rosemary stalks
850g (1¾-pound) smoked ham hock
2 tablespoons olive oil
1 tablespoon smoked paprika
700g (1½ pounds) tomato passata
⅓ cup (80ml) pure maple syrup
char-grilled bread and finely grated parmesan, to serve

1 Place beans in a medium bowl with enough water to cover; stand overnight. Drain. Rinse under cold water; drain well.
2 Peel and finely chop onions and garlic; reserve skins. Remove rosemary leaves from stalks, finely chop; reserve stalks.
3 Place beans, reserved onion and garlic skins, rosemary stalks and ham hock in a large saucepan with enough water to cover. Bring to the boil. Reduce heat to low; cook, covered, for 40 minutes, or until beans are tender. Strain bean mixture through a fine sieve over a large heatproof bowl; reserve cooking liquid. Remove ham hock; finely chop meat. Discard ham bone and vegetable trimmings; reserve beans.
4 Heat oil in a large heavy-based saucepan over medium heat; cook chopped onion, garlic and rosemary for 5 minutes or until softened. Add 1 cup (250ml) of the reserved cooking liquid, ham meat, paprika, passata and maple syrup. Bring to the boil. Reduce heat to low; cook for 10 minutes. Stir in beans; season to taste.
5 Sprinkle baked beans with parmesan; serve with bread.

TIPS Freeze remaining cooking liquid and use to cook rice or as a stock in casseroles and soups. Cook double the recipe and freeze the second batch of beans.

PREP + COOK TIME 1 HOUR 20 MINUTES (+ REFRIGERATION) SERVES 6

PORK & VEAL MEATBALLS
with tomato fennel sauce

This simple Italian meal is great for dinner, using only a handful of ingredients to make a delicious and filling dish. Passata is sieved tomato puree; to substitute, puree and sieve canned tomatoes or use canned tomato puree which is similar, but slightly thicker.

1kg (2 pounds) minced (ground) pork and veal (see tips)
1 cup (70g) fresh breadcrumbs (see tips)
1 cup (120g) finely grated cheddar
2 eggs
1 cup finely chopped fresh flat-leaf parsley
4 cloves garlic, crushed
2 tablespoons olive oil
2 medium onions (300g), chopped finely
1 medium fennel bulb (300g), trimmed, sliced thinly
3½ cups (980g) tomato passata
1 cup (250ml) chicken or beef stock

1 Combine pork and veal, breadcrumbs, cheddar, eggs, parsley and half the garlic in a large bowl; season. Roll rounded tablespoons of mixture into balls. Place on tray, cover; refrigerate for 20 minutes.
2 Preheat oven to 180°C/350°F.
3 Heat 1 tablespoon of the oil in a large heavy-based frying pan over high heat. Add half the meatballs; cook, shaking pan occasionally, for 5 minutes or until browned all over. Transfer meatballs to a 3-litre (12-cup) ovenproof dish. Repeat with another tablespoon of oil and remaining meatballs.
4 Wipe out pan. Heat remaining oil in same pan over high heat; cook onion, fennel and remaining garlic, stirring, for 5 minutes or until softened. Stir in fennel mixture, passata and stock.
5 Bake, covered, for 45 minutes or until fennel is tender. Season to taste.

serving suggestions Serve with linguini, and topped with shaved parmesan.

TIPS Use 500g (1 pound) pork mince and 500g (1 pound) veal or lean beef mince instead, if you like. Fresh breadcrumbs are best made from 2 or 3 day-old bread. Process the bread with crusts into coarse crumbs. This recipe is suitable to freeze at the end of step 4.

PREP + COOK TIME 2 HOURS 30 MINUTES SERVES 8

panang LAMB CURRY

Panang curry is a type of red Thai curry that is thick, salty and sweet, with a nutty peanut flavour; the addition of peanut butter helps to bring out the flavour when using a store-bought curry paste. Serve with steamed jasmine rice.

1 tablespoon peanut oil
1.5kg (3 pounds) boneless lamb shoulder, cut into 5cm (2-inch) pieces
½ cup (150g) panang curry paste
2½ cups (625ml) coconut cream
1 cup (250ml) beef or chicken stock or water
2 tablespoons fish sauce
¼ cup (65g) grated palm sugar
2 tablespoons peanut butter
4 kaffir lime leaves
225g (7 ounces) canned sliced bamboo shoots, drained, rinsed
1 small red capsicum (bell pepper) (150g), sliced thinly
200g (6½ ounces) green beans, trimmed
½ cup fresh coriander (cilantro) leaves

1 Heat oil in a large flameproof casserole dish over high heat; cook lamb, in batches, for 5 minutes or until browned. Return all lamb to dish.

2 Add curry paste to same dish; cook, stirring, for 1 minute or until fragrant. Stir in coconut cream, stock, fish sauce, sugar, peanut butter and lime leaves; bring to the boil. Reduce heat to low; cook, covered, for 2 hours or until lamb is tender.

3 Stir in bamboo shoots, capsicum and green beans; cook, covered, for a further 10 minutes or until vegetables are tender. Season to taste.

4 Serve curry topped with coriander.

TIPS If the curry is too thin at the end of the cooking time, simmer, uncovered, until thickened. If too thick, stir in a little extra coconut cream or stock. This recipe is not suitable to freeze.

PREP + COOK TIME 3 HOURS SERVES 6

beef RENDANG

Rendang is known as a dry curry as it has much less liquid than traditionally found in similar dishes. Our version uses a homemade spice paste, but you can substitute a store-bought paste if short on time. The flavour will not be the same.

2 tablespoons vegetable oil
1kg (2 pounds) gravy beef, cut into 3cm (1¼-inch) pieces
4cm (1½-inch) piece fresh galangal (20g), grated finely
1⅔ cups (400ml) coconut milk
2 x 10cm (4-inch) stalks fresh lemon grass (40g), bruised
1 cup (250ml) water
½ cup (40g) shredded coconut, toasted

spice paste

6 shallots (150g), chopped coarsely
4 fresh long red chillies, chopped
6cm (2¼-inch) piece fresh ginger (30g), grated finely
4cm (1½-inch) piece fresh turmeric (20g), sliced thinly
4 cloves garlic, quartered
3 teaspoons ground coriander

1 Make spice paste.

2 Heat oil in a large heavy-based saucepan over high heat; cook beef, in batches, for 5 minutes or until browned. Remove from pan.

3 Add spice paste and galangal to pan; cook, stirring, for 2 minutes or until fragrant. Return beef to pan, add coconut milk, lemon grass and the water; cover, bring to the boil. Reduce heat to low; cook, covered, for 2 hours or until tender.

4 Discard lemon grass; season to taste. Serve rendang topped with coconut.

spice paste Blend or process ingredients until mixture forms a thick paste.

serving suggestion Serve with steamed basmati rice.

TIPS If fresh turmeric is unavailable, use ½ teaspoon ground turmeric. If you prefer the curry more moist, drizzle with a little warmed coconut milk at serving time. This recipe is suitable to freeze.

PREP + COOK TIME 2 HOURS 25 MINUTES SERVES 4

moroccan LAMB SHANKS

Ras el hanout is a classic spice blend used in Moroccan cooking. The name means 'top of the shop' and is the very best spice blend a spice merchant has to offer. Most versions contain over a dozen spices, including cardamom, nutmeg, mace, cinnamon and ground chilli.

1 tablespoon olive oil
4 french-trimmed lamb shanks (800g)
1 small onion (80g), chopped finely
1 teaspoon ras el hanout
1 teaspoon ground ginger
1 teaspoon ground cinnamon
½ teaspoon ground cumin
½ teaspoon ground white pepper
pinch saffron threads
400g (12½ ounces) canned chopped tomatoes
1½ cups (375ml) vegetable stock
2 tablespoons currants
180g (6 ounces) persian fetta, crumbled
2 tablespoons finely chopped preserved lemon rind
2 tablespoons roasted slivered almonds
¼ cup fresh coriander (cilantro) leaves

1 Preheat oven to 150°C/300°F.

2 Heat oil in a large flameproof casserole dish; cook lamb, turning, for 5 minutes or until browned all over. Remove from dish.

3 Cook onion in same dish, stirring, until softened. Add spices; cook, stirring, until fragrant. Return lamb to dish, add tomatoes, stock and currants; bring to the boil. Transfer to oven; cook, covered, for 2½ hours or until lamb is almost falling off the bone. Season to taste.

4 Skim and discard excess fat from surface of sauce.

5 Divide lamb and sauce among plates. Serve sprinkled with fetta, preserved lemon rind, almonds and coriander.

TIPS Persian fetta is a soft, creamy cheese marinated in a blend of olive oil, garlic, herbs and spices. It is available from most delicatessens and major supermarkets. This recipe can be made a day ahead to the end of step 3.

PREP + COOK TIME 50 MINUTES SERVES 6

SWEET & SOUR PORK STEW
with coconut rice

1 tablespoon cornflour (cornstarch)
1 egg, beaten lightly
2 tablespoons light soy sauce
1kg (2 pounds) pork neck (scotch fillet), cut into 2cm (¾-inch) pieces
2 tablespoons rice bran oil
1 medium red onion (170g), chopped coarsely
30g (1-ounce) piece fresh ginger, cut into matchsticks
4 cloves garlic, sliced
3 fresh long red chillies, sliced thinly
1 medium red capsicum (bell pepper) (200g), chopped coarsely
700g (1½ pounds) fresh pineapple, peeled, core removed, chopped coarsely
2 medium tomatoes (300g), chopped coarsely
¾ cup (180ml) rice wine vinegar
1 cup (250ml) chinese cooking wine (shao hsing)
2½ tablespoons honey
3 green onions (scallions), green tops sliced thinly, white part reserved
½ cup (75g) roasted salted cashews, chopped
1 lime (65g), cut into wedges

coconut rice
1 tablespoon rice bran oil
2 cups (360) brown jasmine rice
400ml canned coconut cream
2½ cups (625ml) water

1 Combine cornflour, egg and soy sauce in a large bowl; add pork, toss to coat. Season. Heat oil in a large saucepan over high heat; cook pork, stirring, for 5 minutes or until browned. Using a slotted spoon, transfer pork to a heatproof bowl.
2 Add red onion, ginger, garlic and chilli to pan; cook, stirring, for 4 minutes or until soft. Add capsicum; cook, stirring, for 3 minutes. Add pineapple, tomato, pork and any pork resting juices, rice wine vinegar, cooking wine and honey to pan. Reduce heat to low; cook for 20 minutes or until sauce has thickened. Season to taste.
3 Meanwhile, make coconut rice.
4 Top coconut rice with pork stew; sprinkle with green onion and cashews. Serve with lime wedges.

coconut rice Finely chop the reserved white part of the green onion. Heat oil in a medium saucepan over high heat; cook chopped green onion, stirring, for 2 minutes or until softened. Add rice; cook, stirring for 1 minute or until coated in oil. Add coconut cream and the water; bring to the boil. Reduce heat to low; cook, stirring occasionally, for 20 minutes or until most of the liquid is absorbed. Remove pan from heat. Stand, covered, for 5 minutes or until rice is tender. Fluff rice with a fork. Season to taste.

PREP + COOK TIME 3 HOURS 45 MINUTES **MAKES** 4

balsamic honey PULLED PORK BUNS

These pulled pork buns are a great casual dinner, or you could use mini brioche buns and serve them as sliders for finger food at your next party. You could use pork scotch fillet (neck) instead of pork shoulder for this recipe, if you like.

800g (1½-pound) piece trimmed pork shoulder
2 tablespoons olive oil
1 large onion (200g), chopped
4 cloves garlic
4 sprigs fresh thyme
2 sprigs fresh rosemary
2 cups (500ml) chicken stock
1 cup (250ml) water
4 brioche buns (280g), split

cabbage & radish coleslaw

200g (6½ ounces) cabbage, sliced thinly
4 trimmed radishes (60g), sliced thinly
2 tablespoons finely chopped fresh chives
¾ cup (150g) mayonnaise
2 tablespoons white wine vinegar

balsamic honey barbecue sauce

3 teaspoons olive oil
1 small onion (80g), chopped finely
2 cloves garlic, crushed
1 cup (250ml) balsamic vinegar
½ cup (140g) tomato sauce (ketchup)
¼ cup (55g) firmly packed brown sugar
2 tablespoons honey
1 tablespoon worcestershire sauce
1 tablespoon dijon mustard

1 Preheat oven to 160°C/325°F.

2 Season pork. Heat oil in a large flameproof casserole dish over high heat; cook pork for 2 minutes on each side or until browned. Add onion, garlic and herbs; cook, stirring, for 2 minutes or until softened. Add stock and the water; bring to the boil. Transfer to oven; cook, covered, for 2 hours. Remove lid; cook for a further 1 hour or until pork is tender.

3 Meanwhile, make cabbage and radish coleslaw.

4 Remove pork from dish, cover with foil; set aside. Strain cooking liquid into a medium bowl; discard solids. Reserve 1 cup of the cooking liquid.

5 Make balsamic honey barbecue sauce.

6 Shred pork, then stir through barbecue sauce. Sandwich buns with shredded pork and coleslaw.

cabbage & radish coleslaw Combine ingredients in a large bowl; season to taste. Refrigerate until required.

balsamic honey barbecue sauce Heat oil in a large saucepan over medium heat; cook onion and garlic, stirring, for 3 minutes or until softened. Add remaining ingredients and reserved cooking liquid; bring to the boil. Reduce heat to low; cook, stirring occasionally, for 15 minutes or until reduced by half. Season.

PREP + COOK TIME 30 MINUTES SERVES 4

pressure-cooked PORK & SAGE STEW

You will need a pressure cooker for this recipe.

1 tablespoon olive oil
800g (1½ pounds) rindless pork belly, chopped coarsely
40g (1½ ounces) butter
1 medium leek (350g), sliced thinly
2 cloves garlic, crushed
⅓ cup (80ml) verjuice
¾ cup (180ml) chicken stock
8 fresh sage leaves
2 medium parsnips (500g), quartered
2 medium firm pears (460g), quartered
¼ cup fresh sage leaves, extra

1 Heat oil in a 6-litre (24-cup) pressure cooker; cook pork, in batches, for 5 minutes or until browned. Remove from cooker.
2 Melt half the butter in cooker; cook leek and garlic, stirring, for about 5 minutes or until leek softens. Return pork to cooker with verjuice, stock and sage; secure lid. Bring cooker to high pressure. Reduce heat to stabilise pressure (see tips); cook for 10 minutes.
3 Release pressure using the quick release method (see tips); remove lid. Add parsnip; secure lid. Bring cooker to high pressure. Reduce heat to stabilise pressure (see tips); cook for 3 minutes. Release pressure using the quick release method (see tips); remove lid. Add pear; secure lid. Bring cooker to high pressure. Reduce heat to stabilise pressure (see tips); cook for 2 minutes.
4 Meanwhile, melt remaining butter in a small frying pan; cook extra sage leaves until bright green and crisp. Drain on paper towel.
5 Release pressure using the quick release method (see tips); remove lid. Season to taste. Serve stew sprinkled with crisp sage leaves.

tips If you have an electric pressure cooker you won't need to reduce the heat to stabilise pressure, as your cooker will automatically stabilise itself. Always check with the manufacturer's instructions before using. For the quick release method referred to above, use tongs (steam can burn your fingers) to turn the pressure valve and release the steam. This will release the pressure quickly, before you remove the lid to either check the food or add more ingredients. Make sure you use firm pears for this recipe or they will become mushy. Stew is suitable to freeze.

serving suggestions Serve with steamed spinach or sugar snap peas and crusty bread to mop up the juices.

PREP + COOK TIME 40 MINUTES SERVES 4

peri coconut PORK CURRY

The Indian region of Kerala is known for its wealth of coconut trees, so it's no wonder that the curry named after the region is rich in coconut flavour. You can cook your own rice instead of using microwave rice, if you prefer. You will need 1 cup (250g) basmati rice.

1 tablespoon olive oil
1kg (2 pounds) pork fillets, cut 5cm (2-inch) pieces
1 medium onion (150g), chopped coarsely
¼ cup (60ml) sweet sherry
225g (7 ounces) keralan coconut curry sauce
120g (4 ounces) peri peri sauce
165ml canned coconut milk
1 cup (250ml) water
2 tablespoons tomato paste
200g (6½ ounces) broccolini, trimmed, halved
⅓ cup (25g) shredded coconut
500g (1 pound) packaged basmati microwave rice
¼ cup loosely packed fresh micro mint
1 teaspoon black sesame seeds

1 Heat oil in a large heavy-based saucepan over high heat; cook pork, in batches, until browned all over.

2 Add onion and sherry to pan with pork; cook, stirring, about 3 minutes or until onion softens. Add sauces, coconut milk, the water and paste; bring to the boil. Reduce heat; simmer, covered, for 15 minutes. Stir in broccolini; simmer, covered, for 10 minutes or until pork is tender and cooked through. Cut pork into thin slices. Return to pan. Season. Cook, uncovered, for a further 5 minutes or until thickened slightly.

3 Meanwhile, stir coconut in a medium frying pan, over low heat, for 3 minutes or until golden. Remove coconut from the pan immediately to prevent over-browning.

4 Microwave rice according to directions on packet. Place rice in a medium bowl with coconut; stir to combine.

5 Top curry with mint and seeds; serve with coconut rice.

PREP + COOK TIME 2 HOURS 45 MINUTES SERVES 8

osso bucco WITH SAFFRON RISOTTO

1 cup (150g) plain (all-purpose) flour
8 x 3cm (1¼-inch) thick veal osso bucco (2kg)
¼ cup (60ml) olive oil
2 medium onions (300g), chopped finely
2 cloves garlic, crushed
4 medium tomatoes (600g), grated coarsely, skin discarded
2 bay leaves
1 cup (250ml) dry white wine
2 cups (500ml) chicken stock
2 teaspoons each finely chopped fresh sage, rosemary and thyme
1 cup (250ml) water

saffron risotto

½ teaspoon saffron threads
¾ cup (180ml) dry white wine
3 cups (750ml) chicken stock
3 cups (750ml) water
90g (3 ounces) butter
1 large onion (200g), chopped finely
2¼ cups (450g) arborio or carnaroli rice
¾ cup (60g) finely grated parmesan

gremolata

2 medium lemons (280g)
½ cup finely chopped fresh flat-leaf parsley leaves
1 clove garlic, crushed

1 Preheat oven to 170°C/340°F.

2 Place flour in a bowl; season with salt and pepper. Coat osso bucco in flour; shake away excess. Heat oil in a large flameproof casserole dish over high heat; cook osso bucco for 2 minutes on each side or until browned. Remove from pan.

3 Cook onion in same pan, stirring over medium-high heat, for 5 minutes or until softened. Add garlic, tomato, bay leaves and wine; bring to the boil. Reduce heat to low; cook for 2 minutes. Add stock, herbs and the water; return osso bucco to pan, stirring to mix well. Bring to the boil. Transfer to oven; cook, covered, turning osso bucco halfway through cooking time, for 2 hours or until meat is almost falling off the bone.

4 Thirty minutes before osso bucco is cooked, make saffron risotto, then gremolata.

5 Spoon risotto into bowls, top with osso bucco. Serve sprinkled with gremolata.

saffron risotto Combine saffron and wine in a small bowl; stand for 5 minutes. Heat stock and the water in a medium saucepan. Melt half the butter in a large heavy-based saucepan over medium heat; cook onion for 5 minutes or until softened. Add rice; stir for 1 minute to coat in mixture. Add wine mixture; cook, stirring, for 3 minutes or until liquid is almost evaporated. Stir in 1 cup of hot stock mixture; cook, stirring, over low heat until liquid is absorbed. Continue adding stock mixture in 1-cup batches, stirring until liquid is absorbed after each addition. Cook for 25 minutes or until all stock has been absorbed and rice is tender. Remove from heat; stir in parmesan and remaining butter. Season.

gremolata Remove rind from lemons with a zester, cutting into thin strips. Combine with remaining ingredients in a small bowl.

TIPS If you don't have a zesting tool, remove the rind thinly with a vegetable peeler then cut each piece into long thin strips. There are different types of risotto rice, each absorbs liquid differently. Take care with arborio as it is easily overcooked, while carnaroli is much more forgiving.

PREP + COOK TIME 3 HOURS 10 MINUTES SERVES 4

fragrant Vietnamese-style BEEF STEW

This is a simple and fresh take on the Vietnamese stew called bò kho, a spicy and warming dish which in Vietnam is traditionally eaten for breakfast. Serve stew with steamed basmati rice, over rice noodles, or with a crusty french baguette to soak up all the juices.

1 tablespoon rice bran oil
1kg (2 pounds) beef chuck steak, cut into 3cm (1¼-inch) cubes
2 medium red onions (340g)
1 stalk fresh lemon grass, bruised, quartered
1 teaspoon chinese five spice
3 whole star anise
2 whole cloves
¼ teaspoon cardamom seeds
5 medium tomatoes (750g), chopped
1 litre (4 cups) water
¼ cup (60ml) fish sauce
2 tablespoons lime juice
1 teaspoon sea salt flakes
2 bunches mixed heirloom baby (dutch) carrots (800g), trimmed, peeled
125g (4 ounces) baby corn, sliced diagonally
1 cup (80g) bean sprouts
1 cup loosely packed fresh thai basil sprigs
1 fresh long red chilli, sliced thinly
1 lime (65g), cut into wedges

1 Heat oil in a large heavy-based saucepan or flameproof casserole dish over high heat. Cook beef, in two batches, for 5 minutes or until browned all over. Remove from pan.

2 Reduce heat to medium. Chop one onion coarsely. Cook chopped onion, stirring, for 5 minutes or until softened. Add lemon grass and spices; cook, stirring, for 1 minute or until fragrant. Stir in tomato; cook, stirring occasionally, for 4 minutes or until softened.

3 Return beef to pan, add the water and fish sauce; season with a little freshly ground black pepper. Bring to the boil, reduce heat to low; cook, covered, stirring occasionally, for 2 hours or until beef is very tender.

4 Meanwhile, slice remaining onion thinly. Combine sliced onion with lime juice and salt in a medium non-reactive bowl. Stand, covered, for at least 1 hour. Drain before using.

5 Add carrots and corn to beef mixture; simmer, covered, for 20 minutes or until vegetables are tender. Season to taste.

6 Top beef stew with bean sprouts, pickled onion, basil sprigs and chilli. Serve with lime wedges.

TIPS If you can't find fresh thai basil, use coriander instead. Stew can be made a day ahead and refrigerated in an airtight container; or freeze for up to 2 months. Make pickled onion on day of serving and add the toppings just before serving.

PREP + COOK TIME 2 HOURS 30 MINUTES SERVES 4

korean braised beef ribs
WITH KIMCHI & DAIKON NOODLES

Kimchi actually refers to any salted and fermented vegetable in Korean cuisine, but by far the most recognisable of these is baechu kimchi, kimchi made with wombok. Koreans are said to eat roughly 18kg of kimchi per person annually.

1 tablespoon vegetable oil
1kg (2 pounds) beef short ribs, cut 6cm (2½-inch) high
1 bunch green onions (scallions) (300g)
1 tablespoon finely chopped fresh ginger
2 cloves garlic, crushed
2 tablespoons sesame oil
2 tablespoons rice wine vinegar
1 tablespoon soy sauce
1 tablespoon gochujang (see tips)
1 litre (4 cups) water
1 cup (100g) kimchi
1 medium firm pear (230g), grated coarsely
100g (3 ounces) fresh shiitake mushrooms
1 large daikon (800g)
500g (1 pound) baby buk choy, quartered lengthways
100g (3 ounces) enoki mushrooms
1 tablespoon sesame seeds
½ teaspoon gochugaru (korean red pepper flakes)

1 Heat vegetable oil in a large heavy-based saucepan or casserole dish over high heat. Season ribs; cook, turning occasionally, for 8 minutes or until browned all over.

2 Chop the white part of the green onions; refrigerate reserved green tops for serving. Add white part of onion, ginger and garlic to pan; cook, stirring, for 30 seconds or until fragrant.

3 Place sesame oil, rice wine vinegar, soy sauce and gochujang in a large jug; whisk until combined. Add mixture to pan with the water, kimchi and pear; bring to a simmer. Cook, covered, over low heat, stirring every 30 minutes, for 2 hours or until beef is tender and falls away from the bone; add shiitake mushrooms to pan for last 30 minutes of the cooking time.

4 Meanwhile, use a julienne peeler, spiraliser, julienne attachment on a mandoline or V-slicer to cut daikon into long thin strips. Cook daikon in a large saucepan of boiling salted water for 3 minutes or until just tender; drain well.

5 Place buk choy and enoki mushroom on top of braised beef rib mixture. Cook, covered, for a further 2 minutes or until vegetables are just tender.

6 Trim the green tops of the onions; cut into long thin strips. Top ribs with green onion; sprinkle with seeds and chilli flakes. Serve with daikon noodles.

TIPS Gochujang is a Korean chilli paste, available from Asian food stores. We used mild gochujang paste; you can use hot if preferred. Recipe can be made to the end of step 3 a day ahead and refrigerated in an airtight container.

TIP The crisp coconut and peanut topping, known as serundeng, is usually sprinkled over a hot dish just as it's served, much like an Italian gremolata, to add a delicious and textual element.

PREP + COOK TIME 1 HOUR 30 MINUTES (+ STANDING) SERVES 6

BEEF CURRY
with coconut rice

2 tablespoons peanut oil
800g (1½ pounds) beef strips
1 medium onion (150g), chopped finely
3 cloves garlic, crushed
1 fresh long red chilli, seeded, chopped finely
10cm (4-inch) stalk fresh lemon grass (20g), chopped finely
1 whole star anise
1 cinnamon stick, halved
4 cardamom pods, bruised
350g (11 ounces) snake beans, cut into 4cm (1½-inch) lengths
2 tablespoons ground bean sauce
2 tablespoons fish sauce
½ cup fresh coriander (cilantro) leaves

coconut rice

1¾ cups (350g) jasmine rice
400ml canned coconut cream
½ teaspoon ground turmeric
1¼ cups (310ml) water

crisp coconut & peanut topping

2 tablespoons peanut oil
2 cloves garlic, crushed
4 green onions (scallions), chopped
3 cups (150g) flaked coconut
2 tablespoons brown sugar
½ cup (150g) tamarind concentrate
10cm (4-inch) stalk fresh lemon grass (20g), chopped finely
1 cup (140g) roasted unsalted peanuts

1 Make coconut rice.

2 Meanwhile, make crisp coconut and peanut topping.

3 Heat half the oil in a wok over high heat; stir-fry beef, in batches, until browned. Remove from wok; cover to keep warm.

4 Heat remaining oil in wok; stir-fry onion for 2 minutes or until soft. Add garlic, chilli, lemon grass, star anise, cinnamon, cardamom and beans; stir-fry for 3 minutes or until beans are almost tender. Return beef to wok with sauces; stir-fry until heated through. Remove from heat; stir in coriander.

5 Stir three-quarters of the crisp coconut and peanut topping through the coconut rice; sprinkle remaining topping over curry. Serve curry with rice and topped with extra coriander, if you like.

coconut rice Soak rice in cold water for 30 minutes. Drain; rinse until water runs clear. Place rice, coconut cream, turmeric and the water in a medium saucepan; bring to the boil, stirring occasionally. Reduce heat to low; cook, covered, for 15 minutes or until liquid is absorbed. Remove from heat; stand, covered, for 5 minutes.

crisp coconut & peanut topping Preheat oven to 150°C/300°F. Heat oil in a wok over medium heat; stir-fry remaining ingredients, tossing continuously, for 15 minutes or until browned lightly. Transfer mixture to a lined-oven tray; roast 20 minutes or until mixture has dried.

PREP + COOK TIME 6 HOURS 45 MINUTES SERVES 4

SLOW-COOKER BALSAMIC LAMB
with polenta & cavolo nero

You will need a slow cooker for this recipe.

¼ cup (35g) plain (all-purpose) flour
½ teaspoon ground cinnamon
pinch chilli powder
2 tablespoons olive oil
1.2kg (2½ pounds) diced lamb leg
1 large red onion (300g), sliced thickly
1 medium carrot (120g), chopped coarsely
1 stalk celery (150g), trimmed, sliced thickly
3 cloves garlic, crushed
½ cup (125ml) dry red wine
1 cup (250ml) beef stock
¼ cup (60ml) balsamic vinegar
¼ cup (55g) firmly packed brown sugar
¼ cup (70g) tomato paste
2 tablespoons dried currants
1 dried bay leaf
250g (8 ounces) cavolo nero (tuscan cabbage), trimmed (see tips)

creamy polenta

2 cups (500ml) chicken or vegetable stock
2 cups (500ml) milk
1 cup (170g) polenta (cornmeal)
30g (1 ounce) butter, chopped
½ cup (40g) grated parmesan

1 Combine flour, cinnamon and chilli in a large bowl; season with sea salt and black pepper.

2 Heat oil in a 4.5-litre (18-cup) slow cooker on sear (HIGH) setting. Coat lamb in flour; shake off excess, reserving excess flour. Cook lamb, in batches, for 5 minutes, turning, or until well browned. Remove lamb from cooker.

3 Reduce cooker to sauté (MEDIUM) setting. Cook onion, carrot, celery and garlic, stirring, for 5 minutes or until vegetables soften. Sprinkle with reserved excess flour; cook, stirring, for 3 minutes. Gradually stir in wine, then stock, vinegar, sugar, paste, currants and bay leaf; bring to the boil.

4 Return lamb to cooker. Cook, covered, on low, for 6 hours. Discard bay leaf; season to taste.

5 Just before serving, make creamy polenta.

6 Coarsely shred 2 cavolo nero leaves. Reserve for serving. Coarsely chop remaining cavolo nero leaves. Add chopped leaves to cooker; cook, covered, on high, for 5 minutes or until cavolo nero wilts.

7 Serve creamy polenta topped with lamb mixture and reserved shredded cavolo nero.

creamy polenta Bring stock and milk to the boil in a large saucepan; gradually add polenta, whisking until mixture comes to the boil. Reduce heat to low; cook, stirring, for 5 minutes or until soft and thick. Stir in butter and parmesan; season to taste. Adjust consistency with a little extra milk, if necessary.

TIPS You will need 1 bunch of cavolo nero for this recipe; you can use kale or silver beet instead. Suitable to freeze at the end of step 4.

PREP + COOK TIME 1 HOUR 45 MINUTES SERVES 4

provencal BEEF STEW

If you wouldn't drink it, don't cook with it: that's the rule of thumb for choosing wine for cooking. Cheap, inferior quality wines will impart a less pleasant flavour than a great drinking wine. Serve a hearty casserole such as this with mashed potato or crusty bread to mop up the sauce.

2 tablespoons extra virgin olive oil
1kg (2 pounds) gravy beef, cut into 2cm (¾-inch) pieces
2 rindless bacon slices (130g), chopped coarsely
1 medium leek (350g), sliced thinly
2 medium carrots (240g), diced
1 stalk celery (150g), trimmed, diced
2 cloves garlic, crushed
400g (12½ ounces) canned crushed tomatoes
1½ cups (375ml) beef stock
1 cup (250ml) dry red wine
2 bay leaves
4 sprigs fresh thyme
6 sprigs fresh flat-leaf parsley
2 medium zucchini (240g), sliced
½ cup (75g) pitted black olives

1 Heat oil in large heavy-based saucepan over high heat. Cook beef, in batches, for 5 minutes or until browned all over. Remove from pan.

2 Cook bacon, leek, carrot, celery and garlic in same pan, stirring, for 5 minutes or until leek softens.

3 Return beef to pan, add tomatoes, stock, wine, bay leaves, thyme and parsley; bring to the boil. Reduce heat to low; cook stew, covered, for 1 hour, stirring occasionally.

4 Add zucchini and olives; cook, covered, for 30 minutes or until beef is tender.

5 Remove and discard thyme and parsley before serving.

serving suggestion Serve with mashed potato, if you like.

Polenta

SOFT POLENTA

PREP + COOK TIME 20 MINUTES SERVES 6

Bring 3 cups milk and 2 cups chicken stock to the boil in a large saucepan. Gradually add 2 cups polenta, stirring constantly. Reduce heat; simmer, stirring, for 10 minutes or until polenta thickens. Stir in an extra 1 cup milk and ¼ cup finely grated parmesan until cheese melts. Season with sea salt and freshly ground black pepper.

TIP This recipe is not suitable to freeze

LEMON THYME POLENTA

PREP + COOK TIME 20 MINUTES SERVES 6

Bring 3 cups milk and 2 cups chicken stock to the boil in a large saucepan. Gradually add 2 cups polenta, stirring constantly. Reduce heat, stir in 2 teaspoons lemon thyme leaves; simmer, for 10 minutes or until polenta thickens. Stir in extra 1 cup milk, 1 teaspoon finely grated lemon rind and ¼ cup finely grated parmesan until cheese melts. Serve topped with extra lemon thyme and finely grated parmesan, if you like.

OLIVE POLENTA

PREP + COOK TIME 20 MINUTES SERVES 6

Bring 3 cups milk and 2 cups chicken stock to the boil in a large saucepan. Gradually add 2 cups polenta, stirring constantly. Reduce heat; simmer, stirring, for 10 minutes or until polenta thickens. Stir in an extra 1 cup milk, 75g (2½oz) coarsely chopped pitted kalamata olives and ¼ cup finely grated parmesan until cheese melts. Season to taste.

CHEESY PESTO POLENTA

PREP + COOK TIME 20 MINUTES SERVES 6

Bring 3 cups milk and 2 cups chicken stock to the boil in a large saucepan. Gradually add 2 cups polenta, stirring constantly. Reduce heat; simmer, stirring, for 10 minutes or until polenta thickens. Stir in an extra 1 cup milk, 150g (4½oz) chunky basil dip and ¼ cup finely grated parmesan until cheese melts. Serve topped with extra grated parmesan, if you like.

PREP + COOK TIME 2 HOURS 30 MINUTES SERVES 10

LAMB *rogan josh*

One of the signature recipes of Kashmiri cuisine, rogan josh was originally brought to the Kashmir region by the Moghuls and now is eaten the world over, and is a favourite of British curry houses. Serve with steamed basmati rice and pappadams.

1 bunch fresh coriander (cilantro)
1½ tablespoons vegetable oil
1.2kg (2½ pounds) boned lamb shoulder, cut into 5cm (2-inch) pieces
2 medium onions (300g), sliced thinly
4 cloves garlic, crushed
⅔ cup (200g) rogan josh curry paste
410g (13 ounces) canned tomato puree
1 cup (250ml) water
1kg (2 pounds) orange sweet potato, cut into 2.5cm (1-inch) pieces
1.2kg (2½pounds) canned chickpeas (garbanzo beans), drained, rinsed
150g (4½ ounces) baby spinach leaves

1 Reserve leaves from coriander; cover, refrigerate for serving. Finely chop coriander stems and roots.

2 Heat 1 tablespoon of the oil in a large heavy-based saucepan over high heat; cook lamb, in batches, for 5 minutes or until browned. Remove from pan.

3 Reduce heat to medium; cook onion and garlic, stirring, for 4 minutes or until onion softens. Stir in chopped coriander stems and roots. Add curry paste; cook, stirring, for 1 minute or until fragrant. Add lamb, puree and the water; stir to combine. Bring to the boil; reduce heat. Cook, covered, over low heat for 1½ hours.

4 Add sweet potato to pan; cook, covered, for 30 minutes or until lamb and vegetables are tender. Stir in chickpeas, spinach and reserved coriander leaves; season to taste.

TIPS You can also cook this recipe in a 180°C/350°F oven for 2 hours. Freeze individual portions of cooled curry in airtight containers for up to 1 month. Thaw overnight in the fridge before reheating.

PREP + COOK TIME 2 HOURS SERVES 8

white bean & LAMB STEW

Lima beans are large, flat kidney-shaped, beige dried and canned beans, also known as butter beans. They have a mealy texture and mild taste, making them an idea addition to soups, casseroles and curries for bulk and some extra fibre.

- 1½ tablespoons olive oil
- 6 pork sausages (500g)
- 700g (1½-pound) boned lamb shoulder, cut into 5cm (2-inch) pieces
- 1 large onion (200g), chopped finely
- 1 small carrot (70g), chopped finely
- 1 celery stalk (150g), trimmed, chopped finely
- 4 cloves garlic, crushed
- 1 bay leaf
- 4 sprigs fresh thyme
- 400g (12½ ounces) canned diced tomatoes
- 2½ cups (625ml) chicken stock
- 2 tablespoons tomato paste
- 1.6kg (3¼ pounds) canned lima beans, drained, rinsed

1 Heat 1 teaspoon of the oil in a large flameproof casserole dish over high heat; cook sausages, turning, until browned. Remove from pan; when cool enough to handle, slice sausages thickly.

2 Season lamb. Heat 3 teaspoons of the oil in same dish; cook lamb, in batches, until well browned. Remove from pan.

3 Meanwhile, preheat oven to 200°C/400°F.

4 Heat remaining oil in same dish over medium heat; cook onion, carrot, celery, garlic, bay leaf and thyme, stirring, for 5 minutes or until onion softens. Return lamb and sausages to dish; add tomatoes, stock and paste. Bring to the boil. Transfer to oven; cook, covered, for 1½ hours.

5 Stir beans into lamb mixture; cook, covered, for a further 10 minutes or until lamb is tender and beans are hot.

6 Discard thyme and bay leaf. Season. Serve stew topped with extra fresh thyme leaves, if you like.

TIPS You could use canned cannellini beans, if you prefer. Freeze individual portions of cooled stew in airtight containers for up to 1 month. Thaw overnight in the fridge before reheating.

PREP + COOK TIME 3 HOURS 40 MINUTES SERVES 4

PULLED BEEF
french-dip sandwich

The french-dip sandwich originated in Los Angeles, USA. It's often served in french bread or baguette, hence the name. Each diner has a small bowl of meat juices to dip the sandwich into.

2 tablespoons olive oil
1kg (2-pound) piece beef chuck, cut into 5cm (2-inch) pieces
1 large onion (200g), sliced
2 cloves garlic, sliced
8 sprigs fresh thyme
2 dried bay leaves
2 cups (500ml) salt-reduced beef stock
¼ cup (60ml) worcestershire sauce
¼ cup (55g) firmly packed brown sugar
1⅓ baguettes
100g (3 ounces) provolone cheese, sliced thinly
¼ cup (70g) mild american mustard, or to taste

1 Preheat oven to 160°C/325°F.

2 Heat oil in a dutch oven or other flameproof casserole dish over high heat. Season beef; cook beef, in batches, for 5 minutes or until browned all over. Remove from pan. Cook onion in same pan for 5 minutes or until softened. Add garlic and thyme; cook for a further 1 minute.

3 Return beef to pan with bay leaves, stock, worcestershire sauce and sugar; bring to the boil. Cover; transfer to the oven. Cook for 3 hours or until beef shreds easily when tested with a fork.

4 Discard thyme and bay leaves. Place beef and onion in a bowl; shred beef with two forks. Strain pan juices into a small saucepan; skim fat from surface and discard.

5 Cut whole baguette into thirds; you will have four baguette lengths. Split rolls lengthways. Place on an oven tray; fill each cut evenly with cheese. Bake for 4 minutes or until rolls are warm and cheese is melted. Divide beef and onion evenly between rolls. Reheat pan juices; season.

6 Drizzle hot rolls with mustard; serve with pan juices for dipping.

serving suggestion Serve with french fries.

TIPS You may find it easier or preferable for diners to spoon the juices over the beef just before eating. Use 4 crusty long bread rolls instead of baguette, if preferred. Beef can be made a day ahead to the end of step 4 and refrigerated; reheat beef, covered, with some of the pan juices.

TIP To remove seeds from a pomegranate, cut pomegranate in half crossways; hold it, cut-side down, in the palm of your hand over a medium bowl, then hit the outside firmly with a wooden spoon. The seeds should fall out easily; discard any white pith that falls out with them.

PREP + COOK TIME 2 HOURS 45 MINUTES **SERVES** 6

BAHARAT-SPICED LAMB
with quinoa & pomegranate

Baharat is an aromatic spice blend and includes some or all of the following: mixed spice, black pepper, allspice, dried chilli flakes, paprika, coriander seeds, cinnamon, clove, sumac, nutmeg, cumin seeds and cardamom seeds. It is used throughout the Middle East.

1½ tablespoons baharat
2 tablespoons olive oil
2 lamb neck fillets (1.25kg)
2 cups (500ml) chicken stock
3 dried bay leaves
½ cup (80g) currants
1 cup (200g) white quinoa, rinsed
2 cups (500ml) water
1 cup (280g) Greek-style yoghurt
1 lebanese cucumber (130g), grated coarsely
1 medium pomegranate (320g), seeds removed (see tip)
1 cup fresh mint leaves
1 cup fresh flat-leaf parsley leaves
½ cup (70g) pistachios, roasted, chopped coarsely

1 Preheat oven to 150°C/300°F.

2 Combine baharat and oil in a medium bowl, add lamb; turn to coat. Season. Heat a large heavy-based frying pan over medium-high heat. Cook lamb for 2 minutes on each side or until browned all over. Transfer to a 20cm x 30cm (8-inch x 12-inch) ovenproof dish.

3 Wipe pan clean with paper towel, add stock, bay leaves and currants; bring to the boil. Pour over lamb. Cover dish tightly with baking paper, then foil. Bake for 2 hours 15 minutes or until lamb is tender. Rest for 10 minutes. Using two forks, shred meat. Skim fat from cooking liquid; reserve liquid.

4 Meanwhile, place quinoa and the water in a small saucepan over medium-high heat; bring to the boil. Reduce heat to low; simmer, covered, for 8 minutes or until tender. Remove pan from heat; stand, covered, for 10 minutes. Fluff with a fork. Season.

5 Combine yoghurt and cucumber in a small bowl. Season to taste.

6 Place quinoa on a plate. Top with lamb, pomegranate seeds, herbs, and pistachios. Drizzle with reserved cooking liquid; dollop with cucumber yoghurt.

serving suggestion Serve lamb with wedges of cinnamon-roasted pumpkin.

PREP + COOK TIME 4 HOURS 45 MINUTES SERVES 8

slow-cooker

RED PORK CURRY

You will need a slow cooker for this recipe.

- 1⅔ cups (400ml) coconut milk
- 1 cup (250ml) salt-reduced chicken stock
- ¼ cup (75g) thai red curry paste
- 2 tablespoons fish sauce
- 3 fresh kaffir lime leaves, shredded finely
- 1.5kg (3 pounds) rindless boneless pork belly, cut into 3cm (1¼-inch) pieces
- 2 large orange sweet potatoes (1kg), chopped coarsely
- 270g (8½ ounces) snake beans, chopped coarsely
- 1 cup fresh thai basil leaves
- 2 fresh long red chillies, sliced thinly
- 1 fresh kaffir lime leaf, shredded finely, extra

1 Combine coconut milk, stock, curry paste, sauce and lime leaves in a 4.5-litre (18-cup) slow cooker. Add pork and sweet potato; cook, covered, on high for 4½ hours or until pork is tender.

2 Skim fat from surface; discard. Place beans on surface of curry; cook for a further 5 minutes. Season to taste.

3 Serve curry sprinkled with basil, chilli and extra shredded lime leaf.

serving suggestion Serve with steamed jasmine rice.

TIPS Ask the butcher to chop the pork belly for you. If you have time, refrigerate the curry at the end of step 1 until cold; this solidifies the fat, making it easier to remove and discard. This recipe is suitable to freeze at the end of step 2.

POULTRY

PREP + COOK TIME 1 HOUR SERVES 4

CHICKEN, FENNEL & onion braise

Chicken maryland is a traditional crumbed-chicken dish in America, but in Australia it refers to a cut of chicken consisting of the leg (drumstick) and thigh in one piece with the skin and bone intact. Squeeze the soft garlic from the skin and serve with the chicken.

4 chicken marylands (1.4kg)
1 tablespoon olive oil
2 medium red onions (340g), cut into eight wedges
2 baby fennel bulbs (260g), trimmed, quartered
1 medium lemon (140g), cut into eight wedges
1 small bulb garlic, halved crossways
2 large fresh rosemary sprigs
1 cup (250ml) chicken stock
2 teaspoons fennel seeds

1 Preheat oven to 200°C/400°F.
2 Cut three small slashes in the thickest part of each maryland; season. Heat oil in a large flameproof roasting pan over medium-high heat; cook chicken, turning, for 6 minutes or until browned all over. Add remaining ingredients to pan.
3 Transfer to oven, cook for 45 minutes or until chicken is cooked through and vegetables are tender.
4 Serve chicken with vegetables and pan juices.

serving suggestion Serve with mashed potato or soft polenta.

PREP + COOK TIME 45 MINUTES SERVES 4

CHICKEN, CHORIZO & chickpea stew

Highly seasoned with garlic and chilli, the Spanish chorizo sausage in this recipe adds a deep smoky and spicy taste. As chorizo are cured, they do not require cooking; serve cold with bread, pickled vegetables and a glass of sherry as tapas or grill or fry and serve hot.

1 tablespoon olive oil
8 chicken thigh cutlets (1.6kg)
1 medium red onion (170g), cut into thin wedges
2 cured chorizo sausage (340g), sliced thinly
400g (12½ ounces) canned chickpeas (garbanzo beans), drained, rinsed
1½ teaspoons smoked paprika
2 cups (560g) tomato passata
1 cup (250ml) chicken stock
250g (8 ounces) cherry tomatoes
1 cup (160g) green sicilian olives
1 tablespoon red wine vinegar
2 tablespoons fresh oregano leaves

1 Preheat oven to 200°C/400°F.

2 Heat oil in a large deep frying pan over high heat; cook chicken, turning, for 6 minutes or until browned all over. Transfer to an oven tray; season. Roast chicken for 30 minutes or until cooked through.

3 Meanwhile, heat same pan over medium heat; cook onion and chorizo, stirring, for 5 minutes or until onion softens. Add chickpeas and paprika; cook, stirring, 1 minute or until fragrant.

4 Add passata and stock; simmer for 5 minutes or until thickened slightly. Add tomatoes and olives; cook for 10 minutes or until tomatoes begin to split and soften. Stir in vinegar; season to taste.

5 Add chicken, skin-side up, and any cooking juices to pan. Serve stew sprinkled with oregano.

TIP This recipe can be made 8 hours ahead; reheat in an ovenproof dish covered with foil in a 180°C/350°F oven 30 minutes or until piping hot.

PREP + COOK TIME 35 MINUTES SERVES 4

CHICKEN WITH WHITE BEANS & pancetta

4 chicken thigh cutlets (800g)
2 tablespoons fresh thyme leaves
1 tablespoon olive oil
8 pickling onions (320g)
2 cloves garlic, sliced thinly
100g (3 ounces) thinly sliced pancetta
2 anchovy fillets
¼ cup (60ml) dry red wine
400g (12½ ounces) canned white beans, drained, rinsed
⅓ cup (25g) finely grated parmesan

1 Using a small sharp knife, cut two 2.5cm (1-inch) slits into each thigh cutlet; fill slits with half the thyme. Season chicken.
2 Heat oil in a large deep frying pan over high heat; cook chicken, skin-side down, for 5 minutes or until browned lightly.
3 Meanwhile, peel onions, leaving root ends intact; quarter onions. Turn chicken, then add onions to pan; cook, covered, for 5 minutes or until onion is soft and browned lightly.
4 Add garlic to pan with pancetta, anchovies and remaining thyme; cook, stirring, until pancetta is crisp. Add wine and beans; bring to the boil. Reduce heat; simmer for 5 minutes or until chicken is cooked through. Season to taste. Sprinkle with parmesan to serve.

serving suggestion Serve with a rocket (arugula) salad.

PREP + COOK TIME 45 MINUTES SERVES 4

turmeric yoghurt CHICKEN & CAULIFLOWER

Turmeric can be bought as the whole root, or ground as a bright orange powder. Traditionally used in curries, it's increasingly recognised for its health benefits. It is rich in curcumin, shown to have anti-cancer and anti-inflammatory properties.

2 tablespoons extra virgin olive oil
4 chicken thigh cutlets (800g)
4 chicken drumsticks (600g)
2 medium onions (300g), sliced thinly
4 cloves garlic, crushed
1 teaspoon ground turmeric
2 teaspoons cumin seeds
½ cup (140g) Greek-style yoghurt, plus extra to serve
½ cup (125ml) chicken stock
2 fresh long red chillies
2 fresh long green chilies
500g (1 pound) cauliflower, cut into florets
½ cup (100g) couscous
½ small red onion (50g), sliced thinly
1 tablespoon white balsamic vinegar
¼ cup fresh coriander (cilantro) leaves

1 Heat oil in a large deep frying pan over medium heat; cook chicken, in batches, for 10 minutes or until browned all over. Remove from pan.

2 Add onion, garlic and spices to same pan; cook, stirring, for 5 minutes or until soft. Stir in yoghurt and stock.

3 Return chicken to pan, bring to a simmer. Reduce heat to low; cook, covered, for 10 minutes.

4 Meanwhile, chop one red and one green chilli, leaving remaining chillies whole. Add whole chillies and cauliflower to pan; cook, covered, for 5 minutes or until cauliflower is tender. Remove pan from heat. Remove chicken, cauliflower and ½ cup liquid from pan; keep warm. Add couscous to centre of pan; cover with a lid. Stand for 5 minutes or until liquid is absorbed. Fluff couscous with a fork; season to taste. Return chicken and cauliflower to pan and drizzle with reserved sauce.

5 Combine red onion and white balsamic in a small bowl; stand for 10 minutes.

6 Top chicken mixture with drained onion, chopped chilli and coriander. Serve with extra yoghurt.

TIPS For a gluten-free version, leave out the couscous and serve with steamed rice, drizzled with the pan juices. Recipe is not suitable to freeze.

PREP + COOK TIME 35 MINUTES SERVES 4

duck RED CURRY

Utilising pre-cooked roast duck, this curry is a speedy version of a traditional Thai red curry, that still packs a punch where flavour is involved. Red curry gets its bright colour from red chilli, but is made up of a multitude of ingredients, such as galangal, shrimp paste and lemon grass.

1 peking-style roast duck (1.2kg) (see tips)
1 tablespoon vegetable oil
⅓ cup (100g) red curry paste
¼ cup (65g) grated palm sugar
2 tablespoons fish sauce
1 tablespoon tamarind concentrate
2 kaffir lime leaves, sliced thinly
3¼ cups (800ml) coconut milk
1 medium red capsicum (bell pepper) (200g), chopped
300g (9½ ounces) gai lan, cut into 5cm (2-inch) pieces
1 cup (140g) frozen peas
1 fresh long red chilli, sliced thinly
¼ cup fresh coriander (cilantro) leaves
1 lime (65g), cut into wedges

1 Remove duck meat using a small sharp knife, keeping skin over breasts intact. Slice breast and shred meat from legs.

2 Heat oil in a wok or large frying pan over medium heat. Cook curry paste; stirring, for 3 minutes or until fragrant. Add sugar, sauce, tamarind and lime leaves; cook, stirring, for 5 minutes or until mixture darkens slightly, then add coconut milk and slowly bring to just below the boil. Add capsicum, gai lan and peas; cook for 3 minutes. Add duck meat; cook for 2 minutes or until just heated through.

3 Top curry with chilli and coriander; serve with lime wedges.

serving suggestion Serve with steamed jasmine rice.

TIPS You can buy peking-style roast duck from Asian food stores and some Chinese restaurants. This recipe is not suitable to freeze.

PREP + COOK TIME 50 MINUTES SERVES 4

green masala CHICKEN CURRY

This is a great sauce for a vegetable curry. Omit the chicken and, in step 3, add chunky chopped vegetables such as pumpkin, potato, sweet potato or cauliflower and drained and rinsed canned chickpeas (garbanzo beans) or lentils. Simmer until vegetables are tender.

2 bunches fresh coriander (cilantro) (130g), roots, stems and leaves chopped coarsely
1 cup loosely packed fresh mint leaves
120g (4 ounces) baby spinach leaves
1 fresh jalapeño chilli (25g), seeds removed, chopped coarsely
4 cloves garlic, chopped
¼ cup (60ml) lemon juice
½ cup (125ml) water
2 tablespoons olive oil
1 medium onion (150g), sliced thickly
8 small chicken thigh fillets (1.2kg)
1½ teaspoons ground turmeric
½ teaspoon ground cinnamon
½ teaspoon ground cardamom
¼ teaspoon ground cloves
1 cup (250ml) canned coconut cream
40g (1½ ounces) baby spinach leaves, extra
⅓ cup (25g) natural flaked almonds, roasted
1 lime (65g), cut into wedges

1 Reserve a handful of coriander leaves and mint leaves for serving. Blend or process remaining coriander and mint with spinach, chilli, garlic, juice and the water until smooth.
2 Heat oil in a large deep frying pan over medium-high heat; cook onion, stirring, for 5 minutes or until starting to brown. Add chicken; cook, turning, for 5 minutes or until chicken is browned on both sides. Add spices; cook, stirring, for 1 minute or until fragrant.
3 Stir in coriander puree and coconut cream; bring to the boil. Reduce heat to low; simmer for 20 minutes or until sauce thickens slightly and chicken is cooked through. Season.
4 Serve curry topped with extra spinach leaves, reserved coriander and mint, almonds and lime wedges.

serving suggestion Serve with steamed brown or basmati rice or warm pappadums.

PREP + COOK TIME 2 HOURS 15 MINUTES SERVES 4

MEXICAN SHREDDED CHICKEN *with beans & corn*

1.6kg (3¼-pound) whole chicken
1 tablespoon olive oil
1 medium onion (150g), sliced thinly
3 cloves garlic, crushed
1 medium red capsicum (bell pepper) (200g), chopped coarsely
1 medium green capsicum (bell pepper) (200g), chopped coarsely
1 corn cob (250g), trimmed, kernels removed
2 tablespoons tomato paste
2 teaspoons ground cumin
2 teaspoons dried oregano
1 teaspoon smoked paprika
1 teaspoon dried chilli flakes
400g (12½ ounces) canned diced tomatoes
2 cups (500ml) chicken stock
800g (1½ pounds) canned kidney beans, rinsed, drained
½ cup loosely packed fresh coriander (cilantro) leaves
8 flour tortillas (400g)
sour cream, to serve

avocado salsa

1 large avocado (320g), chopped coarsely
1 lebanese cucumber (130g), chopped coarsely
125g (4 ounces) cherry tomatoes, quartered
1 tablespoon lime juice
1 green onion (scallion), sliced thinly

1 Pat chicken dry, inside and out, with paper towel. Trim excess fat from chicken.

2 Heat oil in a large saucepan over low heat; cook onion and garlic, stirring, until onion softens. Add red and green capsicum, corn kernels, paste and spices; cook, stirring, for 2 minutes or until fragrant. Add tomatoes and stock to the pan, then add chicken; turn to coat chicken in mixture. Bring to the boil, reduce heat to low; cook, covered, for 1½ hours.

3 Remove chicken from pan; when cool enough to handle, discard skin and bones. Shred chicken meat coarsely.

4 Return meat to pan, add beans and bring to the boil; cook for 3 minutes or until warmed through. Remove from heat; season to taste.

5 Meanwhile, make avocado salsa.

6 Top chicken mixture sprinkled with coriander; serve with avocado salsa, tortillas and sour cream.

avocado salsa Combine ingredients in a small bowl; season to taste.

TIPS You can use 250g (8 ounces) of frozen corn kernels, or a rinsed and drained 400g (12½-ounce) can of corn kernels instead of the fresh kernels if you prefer. Recipe is suitable to freeze.

PREP + COOK TIME 2 HOURS 25 MINUTES SERVES 6

BROWN RICE CONGEE *with fried garlic*

In this congee we ditch the white rice for the more textural and flavoursome brown rice. Brown rice retains the high-fibre, nutritious bran coating that's removed from white rice when hulled, and so retain many of the vitamins and minerals that the hull contains.

6 cloves garlic
1.75 litres (7 cups) water
2 cups (500ml) vegetable or chicken stock
1½ cups (300g) brown rice
2 tablespoons finely chopped fresh ginger
4 green onions (scallions), sliced thinly
200g (6½-ounce) chicken breast fillet
½ cup (125ml) vegetable oil
2 tablespoons tamari
½ cup fresh coriander (cilantro) leaves
2 teaspoons toasted sesame seeds

1 Finely chop 1 garlic clove; thinly slice remaining garlic cloves.
2 Place the water, stock, rice, chopped garlic, ginger and a quarter of the green onion in a large saucepan; bring to the boil. Add chicken; return to the boil. Reduce heat to low; cook, partially covered, for 12 minutes or until chicken is cooked through. Remove chicken from soup; cool for 10 minutes. Shred chicken coarsely.
3 Return soup to the boil. Reduce heat to low; cook, partially covered, for 1½ hours or until rice breaks down and forms a thick porridge consistency.
4 Meanwhile, heat oil in a small saucepan over medium heat; cook sliced garlic for 1 minute or until golden. Remove garlic with a slotted spoon; drain on paper towel. Reserve garlic-infused oil.
5 Add chicken and tamari to rice mixture; stir over low heat until warmed through. Top congee with fried garlic, coriander, seeds and remaining green onion. Serve drzzled with reserved garlic-infused oil.

serving suggestion Serve with steamed asian greens.

TIP For a vegetarian version, omit the chicken and add some tofu. Frying garlic tempers the flavour, bringing out a natural sweetness. Just be careful to fry it quickly as overcooking will make it bitter.

PREP + COOK TIME 40 MINUTES SERVES 4

spanish chicken, SAFFRON & TOMATO STEW

Saffron is one of the most expensive spices in the world by weight, this is because it consists of the dried stigmas of the crocus plant; a kilogram of saffron requires 110,000-170,000 flowers. Available ground or in strands; it imparts a yellow-orange colour to food once infused.

pinch saffron threads
¼ cup (60ml) hot water
4 x 150g (4½-ounce) skinless chicken thigh cutlets
1 medium red onion (70g), sliced thinly
30g (1-ounce) piece salami, chopped coarsely
2 cloves garlic, crushed
800g (1½ pounds) canned cherry tomatoes in tomato juice
400g (12½ ounces) canned cannellini beans, drained, rinsed
⅓ cup (80g) chargrilled capsicum (bell pepper) strips
350g (11 ounces) broccolini, trimmed
2 tablespoons coarsely chopped fresh flat-leaf parsley
4 x 20g (¾-ounce) slices ciabatta

1 Combine saffron and the hot water in a jug.

2 Heat a large deep non-stick frying pan over medium heat. Add chicken; cook, turning, for 6 minutes or until browned all over. Remove from pan.

3 Add onion and salami to pan; cook, stirring, for 3 minutes or until softened. Add garlic; cook, stirring, for 1 minute or until fragrant.

4 Add tomatoes and saffron mixture to pan; bring to the boil. Return chicken to pan. Reduce heat to low; cook, covered, for 25 minutes or until sauce thickens slightly.

5 Add beans and capsicum; simmer, uncovered, for 5 minutes or until chicken is cooked through.

6 Meanwhile, boil, steam or microwave broccolini until tender; drain.

7 Sprinkle stew with parsley; serve with broccolini and torn ciabatta.

TIP You can replace the broccolini with any steamed green vegetable: asparagus, brussels sprouts, beans, broccoli, spinach and zucchini are all good choices.

PREP + COOK TIME 50 MINUTES SERVES 6

coriander chicken & VEGETABLE CURRY

Long chillies are usually mild but can vary in their heat intensity. Adjust the amount of chillies you use (or remove the seeds and membranes from all of them), according to you and your family's tolerance level.

3 fresh long green chillies
1 large onion (200g), chopped
5cm (2-inch) piece fresh ginger (25g), chopped
4 cloves garlic, chopped
1 tablespoon ground coriander
1 tablespoon ground cumin
1 teaspoon salt
1kg (2 pounds) chicken thigh fillets
270ml canned coconut milk
2 cups (500ml) chicken stock
600g (1¼ pounds) orange sweet potato, unpeeled, cut into 2.5cm (1-inch) pieces
300g (9½ ounces) cauliflower, chopped
90g (3 ounces) baby spinach leaves
1 tablespoon sesame seeds
⅓ cup (50g) roasted salted cashews
1 cup (280g) Greek-style yoghurt
½ cup coarsely chopped fresh coriander (cilantro)
¼ cup coarsely chopped fresh mint
1 fresh long green chilli, chopped, extra
¼ cup fresh coriander (cilantro) sprigs, extra
1 lime (65g), cut into wedges

1 Remove seeds from two of the chillies; chop seeded chillies and one whole chilli.
2 To make curry paste, blend chopped chilli, onion, ginger, garlic, spices and salt until smooth.
3 Cut chicken fillets into 4cm (1½-inch) pieces. Heat 2 tablespoons of the coconut milk in a large heavy-based saucepan over medium heat, add curry paste; cook, stirring, for 3 minutes or until fragrant. Add chicken; cook, stirring, for 2 minutes or until combined. Add stock and remaining coconut milk; bring to the boil. Reduce heat to low; cook, covered, for 10 minutes.
4 Add sweet potato to curry mixture; simmer, covered, for 5 minutes. Add cauliflower; simmer, covered, a further 5 minutes or until sweet potato and cauliflower are just tender. Stir in spinach until wilted.
5 Meanwhile, cook seeds and cashews in a heated dry small frying pan, until browned lightly. Remove from pan; cool. Blend seeds and cashews until ground finely. Stir nut mixture into curry with ¾ cup of the yoghurt and the chopped herbs. Season to taste.
6 Drizzle curry with remaining yoghurt; top with extra chilli and extra coriander. Serve with lime wedges.

serving suggestion Serve with steamed basmati or brown rice.

PREP + COOK TIME 3 HOURS 45 MINUTES SERVES 4

chicken with lentils, PORT & PANCETTA

You will need a slow cooker for this recipe.

1 cup (200g) French-style green lentils
2 tablespoons olive oil
8 chicken drumsticks (1.2kg)
2 medium leeks (700g), white part only, sliced thinly
2 medium carrots (240g), halved, sliced thinly
2 stalks celery (300g), trimmed, sliced thickly
100g (3 ounces) sliced pancetta, chopped coarsely
⅓ cup (95g) tomato paste
2½ cups (625ml) port
1½ cups (375ml) chicken stock
4 sprigs fresh thyme
1 cup (120g) frozen peas, thawed
1 tablespoon fresh thyme leaves, extra

1 Rinse lentils well; drain.

2 Heat oil in a 4.5-litre (18-cup) slow cooker on sear (HIGH) setting; cook chicken drumsticks, in batches, turning, for 10 minutes or until browned all over. Remove from cooker.

3 Reduce cooker to sauté (MEDIUM) setting. Cook leek, carrot, celery and pancetta, stirring, for 5 minutes or until vegetables soften. Add paste; cook, stirring, for 3 minutes. Stir in port, stock, thyme and lentils.

4 Return chicken drumsticks to cooker; cook, covered, on low setting, for 3 hours.

5 Discard thyme. Add peas to cooker; stand, covered, for 5 minutes. Season. Serve sprinkled with extra thyme.

serving suggestions Serve with creamy polenta, mashed potato or crusty bread to mop up the juices.

PREP + COOK TIME 3 HOURS 35 MINUTES SERVES 4

ITALIAN-STYLE CHICKEN
with tomatoes & pepperoni

You will need a slow cooker for this recipe.

1 tablespoon olive oil
8 chicken thigh fillets (1.3kg), halved
125g (4 ounces) sliced pepperoni
1 medium onion (150g), sliced thinly
1 teaspoon fennel seeds, crushed lightly
3 teaspoons finely chopped fresh rosemary
2 medium red capsicums (bell peppers) (400g), sliced thinly
400g (12½ ounces) canned diced tomatoes
½ cup (125ml) chicken stock
finely chopped fresh chives, to serve

1 Heat oil in a 4.5-litre (18-cup) slow cooker on sear (HIGH) setting; cook chicken, in batches, turning, for 10 minutes or until browned all over. Remove from cooker.

2 Add pepperoni, onion, fennel seeds and rosemary to cooker; cook, stirring, for 5 minutes or until onion softens. Add capsicum, tomatoes and stock; stir to combine. Cook, covered, on low setting for 3 hours.

3 Increase heat to reduce setting (on HIGH); simmer, uncovered, for 15 minutes or until sauce thickens. Season to taste.

4 Serve sprinkled with chives.

serving suggestions Serve with mashed potato, steamed baby potatoes, steamed green beans or crusty bread.

TIPS Serve with mashed potato instead of bread, if you like. Use skinless chicken thigh fillets, if you prefer. Suitable to freeze at the end of step 3.

PREP + COOK TIME 1 HOUR 50 MINUTES SERVES 4

chicken IN A POT

Cooking chicken in a cast-iron dutch oven will produce tender, juicy chicken. If you don't have one or a casserole dish large enough, use a medium roasting pan and cover tightly with two layers of foil.

- 1.5kg (3-pound) whole chicken, trussed (see tip)
- 30g (1 ounce) butter, softened
- 4 thin slices prosciutto (60g)
- 2 medium leeks (700g), trimmed, cut into 1cm (½-inch) slices
- 2 large carrots (360g), chopped coarsely
- 2 trimmed celery stalks (200g), sliced thickly
- 2 medium parsnips (500g), peeled, chopped coarsely
- 1 fresh rosemary sprig
- 4 fresh thyme sprigs
- 1 cup (250ml) dry white wine
- 1 cup (250ml) chicken stock
- 2 tablespoons lemon juice
- ½ cup fresh flat-leaf parsley leaves, chopped coarsely

1 Preheat oven to 180°C/350°F.
2 Place chicken in a 7-litre (28-cup) casserole dish. Rub butter over chicken breast; cover with prosciutto. Arrange vegetables and herbs around chicken; add wine and stock to dish. Roast, covered, for 1 hour.
3 Remove dish from oven; gently stir vegetables. Remove prosciutto from chicken and place on vegetables. Add lemon juice to dish; spoon some pan juices over chicken. Roast, uncovered, for a further 30 minutes or until chicken is light golden and cooked through.
4 Place chicken on a warm platter with vegetables. Season cooking liquid to taste; spoon over chicken and vegetables. Serve topped with parsley.

tip To truss a chicken, tie it into a neat, compact shape; this helps the chicken cook evenly and keep its shape. Here's how: (1) Lay the chicken breast-side up, cut a small hole in the skin at the base and push the parson's nose (tail) through to close the vent. Pull the skin back over the neck and tuck the wings back so that the wingtips secure the skin; (2) Measure a piece of kitchen string long enough to wrap around the entire chicken. Place the centre of the string over the neck end, take it back across the wings and cross it underneath; (3) Bring the string up to tie the legs securely together, taking the string around the legs twice if necessary.

serving suggestion Serve with creamy mash or couscous and steamed asparagus.

PREP + COOK TIME 4 HOURS 30 MINUTES SERVES 6

apricot CHICKEN

You will need a slow cooker for this recipe.

45g (1½-ounce) packet cream of chicken simmer soup mix
405ml (13½ ounces) canned apricot nectar
6 chicken marylands (2.1kg)
1 medium leek (350g), white part only, sliced thickly
2 cloves garlic, crushed
¾ cup (75g) dried apricot halves
¼ cup (20g) slivered almonds, toasted
fresh micro herbs, to serve (optional)

1 Place soup mix in a 4.5-litre (18-cup) slow cooker. Gradually whisk in nectar until smooth.

2 Remove and discard fat and skin from chicken. Place chicken, leek, garlic and apricots in cooker. Cook, covered, on low, for 4 hours. Season to taste.

3 Sprinkle chicken with almonds and micro herbs, if using, to serve.

serving suggestion Serve with almond couscous and steamed green beans.

TIPS Chicken maryland refers to a cut of chicken consisting of the leg (drumstick) and thigh in one piece with the skin and bone intact. It is available from chicken shops and supermarkets. This recipe is suitable to freeze at the end of step 2.

PREP + COOK TIME 40 MINUTES SERVES 4

moroccan chicken & CHICKPEA CASSEROLE

Moroccan spice mixes often contain a mixture of ground cumin, cinnamon, black pepper, coriander, allspice and cayenne pepper. You should always buy dried spices in small quantities, as their flavour becomes less potent as they age.

- 1.3kg (2¾ pounds) chicken thigh fillets
- 1 tablespoon moroccan spice mix
- 2 tablespoons olive oil
- 400g (12½ ounces) canned chickpeas (garbanzo beans), drained, rinsed
- ½ cup (75g) dried apricots
- 1 large onion (200g), sliced thinly
- 800g (1½ pounds) canned crushed tomatoes
- ½ cup (125ml) chicken stock
- ¾ cup (150g) tri-coloured quinoa, rinsed
- ⅓ cup fresh flat-leaf parsley sprigs

1 Preheat oven to 200°C/400°F.

2 Place chicken and spice mix in a large bowl; rub to coat.

3 Heat half the oil in a large heavy-based frying pan; cook chicken, in batches, until browned on both sides. Transfer chicken to a 4-litre (16-cup) ovenproof dish. Add chickpeas and apricots; stir to combine.

4 Heat remaining oil in same frying pan; cook onion, stirring, for 3 minutes or until softened. Add tomatoes and stock; bring to the boil. Carefully pour tomato mixture over chicken mixture; cover. Transfer to oven; roast for 15 minutes or until chicken is cooked through. Season to taste.

5 Meanwhile, cook quinoa in a large saucepan of boiling water for 12 minutes or until tender; drain.

6 Top casserole sprinkled with parsley; serve with quinoa.

PREP + COOK TIME 1 HOUR 15 MINUTES SERVES 4

balsamic BRAISED CHICKEN

Balsamic vinegar, originally from Modena, Italy, is found widely in major supermarkets, ranging in pungency and quality depending on how, and for how long, it has been aged. Quality can be determined up to a point by price; use the most expensive sparingly.

- 3 stalks fresh flat-leaf parsley
- 3 sprigs fresh thyme, plus extra to serve
- 2 dried bay leaves
- 4 chicken marylands (1.4kg)
- 1 tablespoon olive oil
- 1 large carrot (180g), halved crossways, then halved lengthways
- 1 large onion (200g), cut into thick wedges still attached to root
- 2 celery stalks (300g), trimmed, cut into thirds
- 1½ cups (375ml) white balsamic vinegar
- ¼ cup (60ml) balsamic vinegar
- ½ cup (125ml) chicken stock, heated

1 Tie parsley, thyme and bay leaves using unwaxed kitchen string into a small bundle.

2 Trim any fat from chicken. Cut two slashes in thickest part of the thigh. Season.

3 Heat oil in a large casserole dish over medium heat. Cook chicken, skin-side down, for 8 minutes or until browned. Transfer to a plate.

4 Add carrot, onion and celery to dish; cook, stirring occasionally, for 5 minutes or until starting to brown. Add herb bundle and both vinegars. Bring to the boil. Reduce heat to low; simmer for 10 minutes or until reduced by half.

5 Place chicken on top of the vegetables. Add hot stock; cover, simmer for 45 minutes, or until chicken is just cooked. Stand for 10 minutes. Transfer chicken and vegetables to a serving dish. Return cooking dish to medium heat; bring to the boil. Reduce heat; boil for 5 minutes or until liquid is reduced by a third. Skim fat from surface. Season to taste.

6 Serve chicken and vegetables drizzled with sauce and topped with extra thyme sprigs, if you like.

serving suggestion Serve with wilted silver beet (swiss chard) or rainbow chard leaves.

TIPS Use a dish large enough for chicken to fit in a single layer. This recipe is not suitable to freeze.

PREP + COOK TIME 50 MINUTES SERVES 4

AUTUMN CHICKEN FRICASSEE
with buttermilk scones

20g (¾oz) dried porcini mushrooms
1 cup (250ml) boiling water
1 tablespoon olive oil
4 chicken thigh fillets (680g), cut into thirds
1 large onion (200g), sliced thinly
2 cloves garlic, crushed
4 portobello mushrooms (200g), trimmed, sliced thickly
200g (6½oz) swiss brown mushrooms, quartered
½ cup (125ml) white wine (see tip)
2½ cups (625ml) chicken stock
400g (12½oz) kipfler (fingerling) potatoes, unpeeled, sliced thickly on the diagonal
1 tablespoon fresh thyme leaves
2 tablespoons coarsely chopped fresh sage

buttermilk scones

2 cups (300g) self-raising flour
¼ teaspoon bicarbonate of soda (baking soda)
1 teaspoon sea salt flakes
60g (2oz) cold butter, chopped coarsely
¾ cup (180ml) buttermilk
1 tablespoon fresh thyme leaves
1 tablespoon finely chopped fresh sage
1 tablespoon finely chopped fresh flat-leaf parsley
olive-oil spray

1 Place porcini mushrooms and the boiling water in a small bowl; stand.

2 Meanwhile, heat oil in a flameproof casserole dish or large heavy-based saucepan over high heat. Add chicken; cook for 3 minutes on each side or until golden and caramelised. Transfer to a plate.

3 Reduce heat to medium, add onion; cook, stirring, for 5 minutes or until softened. Add garlic, portobello and swiss brown mushrooms, drained porcini and strained reserved soaking liquid; cook, stirring, for 8 minutes or until mushrooms are softened. Add wine, bring to a simmer; cook for 5 minutes or until reduced slightly.

4 Return chicken to pan, add stock and potato; bring to the boil; reduce heat to low-medium. Cook, covered, for 25 minutes. Remove lid; cook for a further 10 minutes or until chicken and potato are tender and sauce reduces slightly.

5 Meanwhile, make buttermilk scones.

6 Sprinkle chicken fricasee with herbs; season to taste. Serve with buttermilk scones.

buttermilk scones Preheat oven to 180°C/350°F. Grease and line a large oven tray with baking paper. Place flour, soda and salt in a medium bowl; rub in butter. Stir in buttermilk and herbs to make a soft, sticky dough. Place 12 spoonfuls of dough onto lined tray; spray lightly with oil. Bake for 15 minutes or until light golden and cooked through. Transfer to a wire rack to cool.

TIP If you prefer, omit the white wine and replace with extra stock, so you use 2 cups (500ml) chicken stock in total instead and add all the stock at once in step 3.

PREP + COOK TIME 5 HOURS SERVES 4

paprika CHICKEN

You will need a slow cooker for this recipe.

¼ cup (35g) plain (all-purpose) flour
1 tablespoon olive oil
8 chicken thigh cutlets (1.6kg), skin removed
1 medium onion (150g), chopped finely
1 large green capsicum (bell pepper) (350g), chopped finely
¼ teaspoon dried chilli flakes
1 tablespoon paprika
2 tablespoons tomato paste
1 cup (250ml) water
⅓ cup (80g) crème fraîche
fresh micro herbs, to serve (optional)

1 Place flour in a large bowl; season.

2 Heat oil in a 4.5-litre (18-cup) slow cooker on sear (HIGH) setting. Coat chicken in flour; shake off excess. Cook chicken, in batches, for 5 minutes on each side or until browned all over. Remove from cooker.

3 Add onion, capsicum, chilli and paprika to cooker; cook, stirring, for 5 minutes or until vegetables soften. Add paste and the water; stir to combine. Return chicken to cooker. Cook, covered, on low, for 4 hours. Transfer chicken to a plate; cover with foil to keep warm.

4 Stir crème fraîche into cooker. Increase heat to reduce setting (on HIGH); simmer, uncovered, for 10 minutes or until sauce thickens. Season to taste. Return chicken to cooker; coat in sauce.

5 Serve chicken with sauce, sprinkled with micro herbs, if you like.

serving suggestions Serve with cooked egg noodles, pasta or mashed potato.

TIPS Chicken lovely legs or thigh fillets can be used instead of drumsticks, if preferred. Suitable to freeze at the end of step 4.

PREP + COOK TIME 50 MINUTES SERVES 4

chicken tikka WITH CAULIFLOWER RICE

Cauliflower rice is a really great healthy alternative to white rice if you are watching your carb intake, you just need a food processor to break up the florets into rice-sized pieces.

1 tablespoon peanut oil
800g (1½ pounds) chicken thigh fillets, sliced thickly
1 medium onion (150g), cut into wedges
1 large red capsicum (bell pepper) (350g), chopped coarsely
250g (8 ounces) truss cherry tomatoes
⅓ cup (100g) tikka curry paste
2 fresh long green chillies, sliced thinly
300ml light cooking cream
¾ cup fresh coriander (cilantro) leaves

raita

¾ cup (200g) Greek-style yoghurt
1 lebanese cucumber (130g), seeded, chopped finely
1 tablespoon finely chopped fresh mint leaves

cauliflower rice

1 small cauliflower (1kg), stems finely chopped, florets coarsely chopped

1 Heat oil in a large deep frying pan over medium-high heat; cook chicken, in batches, until browned all over. Remove from pan.
2 Add onion, capsicum and tomatoes to same pan, reduce heat to medium; cook, stirring, for 5 minutes or until onion softens. Remove tomatoes from pan; cover to keep warm. Add paste and half the chilli to pan; cook, stirring, for 2 minutes or until fragrant. Return chicken to pan with cooking cream; bring to the boil. Reduce heat to low; cook for 10 minutes or until chicken is cooked through. Remove from heat; return tomatoes to pan.
3 Make raita and cauliflower rice.
4 Top chicken tikka with coriander and remaining chilli. Serve with cauliflower rice and raita.

raita Combine ingredients in a small bowl; season to taste.

cauliflower rice Process cauliflower until finely chopped and resembles rice. Place cauliflower in a large frying pan over medium heat; cook, stirring occasionally, for 10 minutes or until just tender. Season to taste.

beef stock

chicken stock

vegetable stock

fish stock

Stocks

While you can purchase stock from any major supermarket, it's so simple and affordable to make your own, using ingredients that might otherwise end up in the bin.

CHICKEN STOCK

PREP + COOK TIME 6 HOURS 15 MINUTES (+ COOLING & REFRIGERATION) MAKES 3 LITRES (12 CUPS)

Place 2kg (4lbs) chicken bones, 2 tablespoons cider vinegar, 2 coarsely chopped medium onions, 2 coarsely chopped celery stalks, 2 coarsely chopped medium carrots, 8 peeled garlic cloves, 6 fresh flat-leaf parsley stalks, 2 teaspoons black peppercorns and 5 litres (20 cups) water in a large saucepan; bring to the boil. Reduce heat; simmer for 6 hours, skimming the surface occasionally. Strain stock through a muslin-lined sieve into a heatproof bowl; discard solids. Season with sea salt. Cool. Cover; refrigerate until cold. Skim and discard surface fat before using.

FISH STOCK

PREP + COOK TIME 25 MINUTES (+ COOLING & REFRIGERATION) MAKES 2 LITRES (8 CUPS)

Place 1.5kg (3lbs) fish bones, 3 litres (12 cups) water, 1 coarsely chopped onion, 2 coarsely chopped celery stalks, 6 fresh flat-leaf parsley stalks and 1 teaspoon black peppercorns in a large saucepan; bring to the boil. Reduce heat; simmer for 30 minutes. Strain stock through a muslin-lined sieve into heatproof bowl; discard solids. Season with sea salt and 2 tablespoons lemon juice. Cool. Cover; refrigerate until cold. Skim and discard any surface fat before use.

BEEF STOCK

PREP + COOK TIME 8 HOURS 15 MINUTES (+ COOLING & REFRIGERATION) MAKES 2 LITRES (8 CUPS)

Preheat oven to 200°C/400°F. Roast 2kg (4lbs) beef bones on a large oven tray for 1 hour or until browned. Place bones in a large saucepan with 2 chopped unpeeled onions, 2 coarsely chopped celery stalks, 2 coarsely chopped medium carrots, 8 peeled garlic cloves, 2 tablespoons cider vinegar, 2 teaspoons black peppercorns and 5 litres (20 cups) water; bring to the boil. Reduce heat; simmer for 8 hours, skimming the surface occasionally. Strain stock through a muslin-lined sieve into a heatproof bowl; discard solids. Add extra water to make up 2 litres. Season with sea salt. Cool. Cover; refrigerate until cold. Skim and discard surface fat before using.

VEGETABLE STOCK

PREP + COOK TIME 1 HOUR 45 MINUTES (+ COOLING & REFRIGERATION) MAKES 3 LITRES (12 CUPS)

Place 4 coarsely chopped unpeeled onions, 2 coarsely chopped large unpeeled carrots, 8 coarsely chopped celery stalks, 2 coarsely chopped large parsnips, 8 peeled garlic cloves, 6 fresh flat-leaf parsley stalks, 2 teaspoons black peppercorns and 4 litres (16 cups) water in a large saucepan; bring to the boil. Reduce heat; simmer for 1½ hours. Add 200g (6½oz) coarsely chopped cup mushrooms and 4 coarsely chopped unpeeled tomatoes; simmer for a further 30 minutes. Strain stock through a muslin-lined sieve into a heatproof bowl; discard solids. Season with sea salt. Cool. Cover; refrigerate until cold.

PREP + COOK TIME 3 HOURS 15 MINUTES SERVES 8

CHICKEN, CHORIZO & okra gumbo

1.5kg (3-pound) whole chicken
2 medium carrots (240g), chopped coarsely
2 celery stalks (300g), trimmed, chopped coarsely
2 medium onions (300g), 1 chopped coarsely, 1 chopped finely
12 black peppercorns
1 dried bay leaf
3 litres (12 cups) water
60g (2 ounces) butter
1 small onion (80g), chopped finely
2 cloves garlic, crushed
1 medium red capsicum (bell pepper) (200g), chopped finely
2 teaspoons dried oregano
1 teaspoon sweet paprika
¼ teaspoon cayenne pepper
¼ teaspoon ground cloves
¼ cup (35g) plain (all-purpose) flour
¼ cup (70g) tomato paste
400g (12½ ounces) canned crushed tomatoes
100g (3 ounces) fresh okra, halved diagonally
1 cup (200g) white medium-grain rice
1 cured chorizo sausage (170g), sliced thinly

1 Place chicken in a large saucepan with carrot, celery, coarsely chopped onion, peppercorns, bay leaf and the water; bring to the boil. Reduce heat to low; cook, covered, for 1½ hours.

2 Remove chicken from pan. Strain broth through muslin-lined sieve or colander into large heatproof bowl; discard solids. When chicken is cool enough to handle, remove and discard skin and bones; shred meat coarsely.

3 Melt butter in a large saucepan over medium heat; cook finely chopped onion and garlic, stirring, until onion softens. Add capsicum, oregano and spices; cook, stirring, for 3 minutes or until fragrant. Add flour and paste; cook, stirring, for 1 minute. Gradually stir in reserved broth and tomatoes; bring to the boil, stirring. Stir in okra and rice; cook, stirring occasionally, for 15 minutes or until rice is tender.

4 Heat a large oiled frying pan; cook sausage until browned; drain on paper towel.

5 Add sausage and chicken to gumbo; stir over medium heat until hot. Season to taste.

TIPS If you want to cook this gumbo a day ahead, the flavours will meld and deepen, making the soup even more delicious. Follow the recipe through to the end of step 2, then cool the stock, cover and refrigerate overnight.

PREP + COOK TIME 1 HOUR 5 MINUTES
(+ STANDING & REFRIGERATION) SERVES 4

healthy BUTTER CHICKEN

1 cup (150g) raw cashews, plus extra to serve
6 chicken drumsticks (900g) (see tip)
600ml buttermilk
2 tablespoons turmeric
1 tablespoon ground cumin
1 tablespoon ground cinnamon
1 tablespoon ground coriander
1 tablespoon sweet paprika
¾ teaspoon ground cloves
1 tablespoon olive oil
1 large onion (200g), chopped coarsely
2 tablespoons tomato paste
1 medium orange sweet potato (400g), cut into 2cm (¾-inch) rounds
1 medium swede (225g), cut into 2cm (¾-inch) wedges
3 cups (750ml) chicken stock
2 trimmed, cleaned corn cobs (500g), cut into 2cm (¾-inch) rounds
60g (2 ounces) watercress sprigs

1 Place cashews in a medium bowl, cover with cold water; stand for 30 minutes or until plump and pale in colour.

2 Meanwhile, place chicken, buttermilk and spices in a large bowl; stir well to coat chicken completely. Cover; refrigerate for 30 minutes.

3 Drain chicken; reserve marinade. Heat oil in a large heavy-based saucepan over high heat; cook chicken for 2 minutes on each side or until fragrant.

4 Add onion to pan; cook, stirring, for 2 minutes or until starting to become soft. Stir in tomato paste and reserved marinade; cook for 2 minutes or until mixture comes to a simmer and is fragrant.

5 Add sweet potato, swede and stock to pan; stir to combine. Bring to the boil, reduce heat to low; cook, covered, for 35 minutes or until chicken is falling off the bone and vegetables are tender when a small knife is inserted. Add corn during the last 10 minutes of cooking time.

6 Meanwhile, drain cashews; reserve ½ cup of soaking liquid. Process cashews and reserved liquid until a smooth paste forms (use a high-powered blender, if you have one, this will achieve a very smooth result).

7 Stir in cashew paste until well combined to thicken sauce; cook, uncovered, for a further 5 minutes or until sauce thickens and coats the back of a wooden spoon. Season to taste.

8 Serve butter chicken topped with watercress; sprinkled with extra cashews.

serving suggestion Serve with warmed naan and steamed basmati rice, if you like.

PREP + COOK TIME 1 HOUR 35 MINUTES SERVES 4

CHICKEN, WHITE WINE & potato casserole

If you wouldn't drink it, don't cook with it: that's the rule of thumb for choosing wine for cooking. Cheap, inferior quality wines will impart a less pleasant flavour than a great drinking wine.

1 tablespoon olive oil
4 chicken drumsticks (600g)
4 chicken thigh cutlets (800g)
1 large onion (200g), chopped finely
4 medium potatoes (800g), quartered
½ cup (80g) roasted pine nuts
½ cup (80g) roasted blanched almonds
3 cups (750ml) chicken stock
1 cup (250ml) dry white wine
⅓ cup (80ml) lemon juice
4 cloves garlic, crushed
2 tablespoons fresh thyme leaves
½ cup coarsely chopped fresh flat-leaf parsley
500g (1 pound) baby green beans, trimmed

1 Preheat oven to 180°C/350°F.

2 Heat oil in a large flameproof casserole dish over high heat; cook chicken, in batches, for 5 minutes or until browned. Remove from dish.

3 Cook onion in same dish, stirring, for 5 minutes or until softened. Return chicken to dish, add potato, nuts, stock, wine, juice, garlic, thyme and half the parsley; bring to the boil. Transfer to oven; cook, covered, for 1 hour or until chicken is cooked through.

4 Meanwhile, boil, steam or microwave beans until tender; drain.

5 Top chicken with remaining parsley; serve with beans.

TIPS Carlingford, desiree, kestrel or mondial potatoes are good varieties to use in this dish. This dish is not suitable to freeze.

PREP + COOK TIME 35 MINUTES SERVES 4

fragrant chicken & RICE NOODLES

Coconut water is the liquid from the centre of a young green coconut. It has fewer kilojoules than fruit juice, with no fat or protein. There are sugars present, but these are slowly absorbed giving coconut water a low GI.

1 litre (4 cups) coconut water (see tips)
1 tablespoon finely grated ginger
2 cloves garlic, chopped finely
¼ cup (60ml) fish sauce
30g (1 ounce) palm sugar, grated coarsely
300g (9½ ounces) chicken breast fillets
600g (1¼ pounds) cooked rice noodles
2 lebanese cucumbers (260g), halved lengthways, sliced thinly on the diagonal
4 green onions (scallions), sliced thinly
2 cups (160g) bean sprouts
¾ cup fresh coriander (cilantro) leaves
¾ cup fresh mint leaves
½ cup fresh thai basil leaves
1 fresh long red chilli, sliced thinly on the diagonal
⅓ cup (45g) toasted slivered almonds
lime wedges, to serve

1 Bring coconut water, ginger, garlic, fish sauce and sugar to the boil in a large saucepan. Add chicken; return to the boil. Reduce heat to low; cook, covered, for 12 minutes or until chicken is cooked through. Remove chicken; cool for 10 minutes. Shred chicken coarsely.

2 Return broth mixture to the boil. Reduce heat to medium; simmer, uncovered, for 10 minutes or until broth has reduced slightly. Remove from heat.

3 Add shredded chicken and noodles to broth; stand for 5 minutes or until warmed through. Divide mixture among bowls; top with cucumber, green onion, sprouts, herbs, chilli and almonds. Serve with lime wedges.

TIPS Make sure you buy pure coconut water that hasn't been sweetened. To make this vegetarian, use soy sauce or salt instead of fish sauce and replace chicken with mixed asian mushrooms.

PREP + COOK TIME 1 HOUR 30 MINUTES SERVES 4

COQ AU VIN

Literally meaning 'rooster in wine', this is a quintessential French peasant dish. Braising slowly for hours was a favourite way of transforming tougher, less common meats (such as rooster) into a hearty, nourishing meal.

750g (1½ pounds) spring onions
¼ cup (60ml) extra virgin olive oil
4 rindless bacon slices (390g), chopped coarsely
310g (10½ ounces) button mushrooms
2 cloves garlic, crushed
8 chicken thigh fillets (880g)
¼ cup (35g) plain (all-purpose) flour
2 cups (500ml) dry red wine
1½ cups (375ml) chicken stock
2 tablespoons tomato paste
3 bay leaves
4 sprigs fresh thyme
2 sprigs fresh rosemary

1 Trim green ends from spring onions, leaving about 4cm (1½ inches) of stem attached; trim roots. Heat 1 tablespoon of oil in large heavy-based frying pan; cook onions, stirring, for 5 minutes or until browned all over; transfer to a large bowl.

2 Add bacon, mushrooms and garlic to pan. Cook, stirring, until bacon is crisp and mushrooms lightly browned; transfer to bowl with onions.

3 Coat chicken in flour; shake off excess. Heat remaining oil in same pan. Cook chicken, in batches, turning occasionally, for 8 minutes or until browned all over; drain on paper towel.

4 Return chicken, bacon mixture and onions to pan; add wine, stock, paste, bay leaves, thyme and rosemary. Bring to the boil; reduce heat to low, cook for 35 minutes or until chicken is tender and sauce has thickened slightly.

TIP Serve this classic French braised chicken with mashed potato or toasted sourdough bread to mop up the juices, if you like.

SEAFOOD

PREP + COOK TIME 1 HOUR SERVES 4

FISHERMAN'S STEW
with turmeric rouille

1 tablespoon olive oil
1 medium onion (150g), sliced thickly
2 cloves garlic, sliced thinly
2 baby fennel bulbs (260g), sliced thinly, fronds reserved
1 fresh long red chilli, sliced thinly
pinch saffron threads
1 bay leaf
2 cups (500ml) salt-reduced vegetable stock
2 cups (500ml) water
400g (12½ ounces) canned cherry tomatoes
2 blue swimmer crabs (650g), quartered, cleaned
300g (9½ ounces) firm white fish fillet, cut into 4cm (1½-inch) pieces
8 large uncooked prawns (shrimp) (560g), peeled and deveined, tails intact
2 medium calamari (320g), cleaned, sliced, legs reserved

turmeric rouille

2 free-range egg yolks
1 clove garlic, chopped coarsely
2 teaspoons white balsamic vinegar
1 teaspoon dijon mustard
½ teaspoon finely grated fresh turmeric
1 cup (250ml) extra virgin olive oil

1 Heat oil in large heavy-based saucepan over medium-high heat; cook onion, garlic and fennel, stirring, for 5 minutes or until softened. Add chilli, saffron and bay leaf; cook, stirring for 2 minutes or until fragrant. Add stock, the water and tomatoes; bring to the boil. Reduce heat to low; cook, covered, for 30 minutes.

2 Meanwhile, make turmeric rouille.

3 Add crab, fish, prawns and calamari to pan; cook, covered, for 8 minutes or until seafood is just cooked.

4 Top stew with reserved fennel fronds; serve with turmeric rouille.

turmeric rouille Process yolks, garlic, vinegar, mustard and turmeric in a small food processor until smooth. Gradually add oil in a thin stream until mixture is thick. Season to taste.

TIP Use a tiny pinch of saffron powder instead of threads, if you like.

PREP + COOK TIME 1 HOUR SERVES 4

seafood STEW

Bouillabaisse, by any other name, was created by the fishermen of Marseille from the items of the daily catch that weren't sold to restaurants. The recipe varies, depending on what fish and shellfish are available on the day of cooking.

4 cleaned baby squid hoods (480g)
2 baby fennel bulbs (260g)
2 tablespoons lemon juice
1 tablespoon olive oil
2 medium onions (300g), chopped finely
4 cloves garlic, crushed
3 x 5cm (2-inch) pieces orange rind
1 fresh long red chilli, chopped finely
pinch saffron threads
⅓ cup (80ml) dry white wine
800g (1½ pounds) canned diced tomatoes
1 litre (4 cups) fish stock
1kg (2 pounds) large uncooked king prawns (shrimp), peeled, deveined, with tails intact
200g (6½ ounces) pipis, scrubbed
250g (8 ounces) small black mussels, scrubbed, beards removed
200g (6½ ounces) baby octopus, cleaned
2 tablespoons thin strips orange rind, extra

1 Insert a large knife into a squid hood. Using a small sharp knife, cut 1cm (½-inch) thick slices on one side of squid. Repeat with remaining hoods.

2 Trim fennel; reserve fronds. Using a mandoline or V-slicer, cut fennel into very thin slices. Place fennel and juice in a small bowl; toss to coat.

3 Heat oil in a large saucepan; cook onion, stirring, until soft. Add garlic; cook, stirring, for 1 minute.

4 Stir rind, chilli, saffron and wine into onion mixture; cook, stirring, for 2 minutes. Add tomatoes; simmer for 10 minutes or until mixture thickens slightly. Add stock; simmer for 20 minutes or until liquid is reduced by about a quarter.

5 Add squid, prawns, pipis, mussels and octopus to pan. Cover; simmer, stirring occasionally, for 5 minutes or until seafood is cooked.

6 Serve stew topped with fennel mixture, reserved fennel fronds and extra rind.

TIP Some mussels might not open. Not all farmed mussels open up during cooking, even after excessive cooking – you do not have to discard these, just open carefully with a knife and cook a little more, if you wish.

PREP + COOK TIME 1 HOUR 35 MINUTES SERVES 4

MUSSELS IN CHILLI BROTH *with freekeh*

Some mussels might not open, even after excessive cooking – you do not have to discard these, just open carefully with a knife and cook a little more, if you wish.

1 cup (250ml) dry white wine
1kg (2 pounds) black mussels, scrubbed, beards removed
1 tablespoon olive oil
1 medium onion (150g), chopped finely
2 celery stalks (300g), trimmed, cut into 1cm (½-inch) pieces
400g (12½ ounces) baby (dutch) carrots, sliced thinly on the diagonal
2 tablespoons tomato paste
1 cup (170g) wheat freekeh, rinsed (see tips)
½ teaspoon dried chilli flakes
3 cups (750ml) fish stock
2 tablespoons coarsely chopped fresh flat-leaf parsley leaves
lemon wedges, to serve

1 Bring wine to the boil in a large heavy-based saucepan over medium-high heat. Add mussels; cook, covered, for 8 minutes or until mussels open. Drain mussels in a colander over a large heatproof bowl; reserve cooking liquid. Transfer mussels to a heatproof bowl, cover; set aside until required.
2 Heat oil in same pan over medium heat; cook onion, celery and carrots for 3 minutes or until onion softens. Add paste, freekeh and chilli; cook, stirring, for 1 minute or until fragrant. Add stock and reserved cooking liquid; bring to the boil. Reduce heat; simmer, partially covered, for 1 hour or until freekeh is tender.
3 Return mussels to pan; cook for 2 minutes or until heated through. Top mussels with parsley; serve with lemon wedges.

TIPS You can use vongole (clams) instead of the mussels, if you like. Freekeh is an ancient grain food made from roasted young green wheat, so it does contain gluten. Freekeh is available at health food shops, some supermarkets, delis and greengrocers.

PREP + COOK TIME 40 MINUTES SERVES 6

keralan fish, SWEET POTATO & EGG CURRY

Good choices of firm white fish for this recipe are pacific john dory, barramundi, ling and snapper. The curry sauce can be made a day ahead. Reheat the sauce and add raw fish just before you are ready to serve.

800g (1½ pounds) firm white fish fillets, cut into 5cm (2-inch) pieces
1½ tablespoons ground turmeric
1 medium orange sweet potato (400g), halved lengthways, sliced thickly
2 tablespoons rice bran oil
2 medium onions (300g), sliced thinly
15g (½-ounce) piece fresh ginger, cut into matchsticks
¼ cup fresh curry leaves
2 fresh long red chillies, sliced thinly
800ml canned coconut milk
1 cup (250ml) water
1 tablespoon tamarind concentrate
1 tablespoon fish sauce
2 teaspoons lime juice
500g (1 pound) packaged microwave brown rice
2 hard-boiled eggs, halved

1 Combine fish and half the turmeric in a medium bowl; refrigerate until required.

2 Meanwhile, boil, steam or microwave sweet potato until tender; drain.

3 Heat oil in a large heavy-based saucepan over low heat; cook onion, covered, stirring occasionally, for 5 minutes or until softened (do not brown). Add ginger, 2 tablespoons curry leaves, half the chilli and remaining turmeric; cook, stirring, for 1 minute or until fragrant.

4 Add coconut milk, the water, tamarind, fish sauce and juice; bring to the boil. Add fish and sweet potato; return curry mixture to the boil. Reduce heat to low-medium; cook for 3 minutes or until fish is just cooked through.

5 Heat rice following packet instructions.

6 Top curry with egg, remaining chilli and remaining curry leaves. Serve with rice.

PREP + COOK TIME 20 MINUTES (+ STANDING) SERVES 4

MUSSELS AND PIPIS *with ginger & lime*

You can use 2kg (4 pounds) mussels if you can't find pipis at your local fishmonger, and use regular basil instead of thai basil, if you prefer.

- 1kg (2 pounds) pipis, scrubbed
- 1 cup (250ml) salt-reduced vegetable or chicken stock
- 7 kaffir lime leaves
- 1kg (2 pounds) small black mussels, scrubbed, beards removed
- 2 tablespoons vegetable oil
- 2 cloves garlic, crushed
- 1 fresh long red chilli, chopped finely
- 20g (¾-ounce) piece fresh ginger, cut into thin matchsticks
- 4 kaffir lime leaves, extra, shredded
- 1 tablespoon fish sauce
- 1 tablespoon oyster sauce
- 1 cup fresh coriander (cilantro) leaves, chopped coarsely
- 1 cup fresh thai basil leaves, sliced thinly

1 Place pipis in a large bowl of cold water; stand for 3 minutes. Drain well.

2 Heat a wok over high heat, add pipis, stock and 3 of the torn lime leaves; cook, covered, stirring occasionally, for 5 minutes or until pipis begin to open. Remove pipis with tongs as they open; use a knife to open any pipis that may remain closed. Repeat process with mussels.

3 Strain remaining stock mixture through a fine sieve into a small heatproof bowl; discard solids. Reserve stock.

4 Finely shred remaining lime leaves. Heat oil in wok over high heat; cook garlic, chilli, ginger and shredded lime leaves, stirring occasionally, for 1 minute or until fragrant. Add sauces and 1 cup (250ml) of the reserved stock; cook, stirring, for 2 minutes or until thickened slightly. Add pipis and mussels; cook, stirring for 1 minute or until heated through. Stir in herbs, serve immediately.

serving suggestion Serve with cooked thai red rice or black rice, both can be found at Asian supermarkets.

TIP Some mussels might not open. Not all farmed mussels open up during cooking, even after excessive cooking – you do not have to discard these, just open carefully with a knife and cook a little more, if you wish.

Grains

BASIC QUINOA

PREP + COOK TIME 20 MINUTES SERVES 4

Rinse 1 cup (200g) tri-coloured quinoa in a sieve under cold running water. Place quinoa and 2 cups (500ml) water in a medium saucepan; bring to the boil. Reduce heat to low; cook, covered, for 15 minutes or until tender. Drain; cool slightly. Season to taste.

PINE NUT & PARSLEY QUINOA

PREP + COOK TIME 20 MINUTES SERVES 4

Place 1 cup quinoa and 2 cups water in a medium saucepan; bring to the boil. Reduce heat to low; cook, covered, for 12 minutes or until the water is absorbed and quinoa is tender. Stir in ⅓ cup toasted pine nuts, 2 teaspoons finely grated lemon rind, 2 tablespoons lemon juice and ½ cup finely chopped fresh flat-leaf

LEMON PISTACHIO COUSCOUS

PREP + COOK TIME 15 MINUTES SERVES 4

Combine 1 cup couscous, ¾ cup boiling water, 2 teaspoons finely grated lemon rind and ¼ cup lemon juice in a heatproof bowl. Cover; stand for 5 minutes or until liquid is absorbed; fluff with a fork. Meanwhile, cook ½ cup pistachios in a dry heated frying pan until fragrant; remove nuts from pan, chop coarsely. Heat 2 teaspoons olive oil in same pan, add 1 crushed garlic clove and 1 finely chopped small red onion; cook, stirring, until onion softens. Fluff couscous then stir through pistachios, onion mixture and ½ cup shredded fresh mint.

PRESERVED LEMON & OLIVE COUSCOUS

PREP + COOK TIME 15 MINUTES SERVES 6

Combine 1¼ cups couscous, 1¼ cups boiling water and 1 tablespoon oil in a heatproof bowl, cover; stand for 5 minutes or until water is absorbed, fluffing with a fork occasionally. Stir 400g (12½oz) drained and rinsed canned chickpeas, ½ cup coarsely chopped pitted green olives, 2 tablespoons lemon juice, 3 thinly sliced green onions (scallions), 2 tablespoons finely chopped fresh flat-leaf parsley and 1 tablespoon thinly sliced preserved lemon rind into the couscous. Season to taste.

PREP + COOK TIME 25 MINUTES SERVES 4

FISH CURRY

Red emperor is one of Australia's most highly regarded fish, with lovely firm white flesh, large flake and a delicate flavour. You could use any firm white fish fillet in this recipe, such as blue-eye trevalla, ling, bream or snapper, if you prefer.

2 tablespoons peanut oil
⅓ cup (100g) yellow curry paste
1 tablespoon fish sauce
4 kaffir lime leaves, torn
2 fresh long red chillies, sliced thinly diagonally
400ml canned coconut cream
2 tablespoons unrefined sugar (see tips)
2 tablespoons lime juice
5 medium apple eggplant (200g), halved
500g (1 pound) red emperor fillets, pin-boned, cut into thirds
300g (9½ ounces) baby buk choy, trimmed, halved
fresh thai basil leaves and lime wedges, to serve

1 Heat oil in a wok or medium heavy-based saucepan over medium heat. Add curry paste; cook, stirring, for 2 minutes or until fragrant.
2 Add fish sauce, lime leaves and chilli; cook, stirring for 1 minute or until fragrant. Add coconut cream; bring to the boil. Reduce heat to low.
3 Stir in sugar, lime juice and eggplant. Bring to the boil. Add fish; simmer for 3 minutes or until fish is cooked. Add buk choy; stir until just wilted.
4 Top curry with basil; serve with lime wedges.

serving suggestion Serve with steamed brown rice.

TIPS We used panela sugar, but any unrefined sugar can be used. If you can't find apple eggplants, use 1 small eggplant, cut into 5cm (2-inch) pieces, instead.

PREP + COOK TIME 15 MINUTES SERVES 2

MUSSELS WITH *cider*

Alcohol is often used to cook mussels in, along with cream, and in this recipe we use apple cider, rather than wine or beer, to add a sweeter note to the dish. This simple recipe is comprised of only 6 ingredients and can be on the table in less than 20 minutes.

340ml bottle cider
1 clove garlic, crushed
1kg (2 pounds) black mussels, scrubbed, beards removed
1 cup (250ml) pouring cream
1 medium zucchini (120g), cut into long matchsticks (see tips)
1 tablespoon fresh tarragon leaves
¼ cup finely chopped fresh chives

1 Bring cider to the boil in a large heavy-based saucepan. Add garlic and mussels; cover, cook, shaking pan occasionally, for 3 minutes or until mussels open (see tips). Transfer mussels to a serving bowl.
2 Stir cream into pan; bring to the boil. Reduce heat to low; simmer, uncovered, for 5 minutes or until thickened slightly. Add zucchini and herbs; season. Spoon sauce over mussels; serve.

serving suggestion Serve with a rocket (arugula) salad and crusty bread.

TIPS Use a mandoline or V-slicer with a julienne attachment to cut the zucchini. Some mussels might not open. Not all mussels open up during cooking, even after excessive cooking – you do not have to discard these, just open carefully with a knife and cook a little more, if you wish.

TIP A tagine is both the name of the dish and the traditional earthenware vessel which is used for cooking it in. The vessel has a flat-bottomed base and a conical lid, designed to trap the steam and keep the food moist. An enamelled cast-iron pan that holds the heat evenly is a good alternative.

PREP + COOK TIME 40 MINUTES (+ REFRIGERATION) SERVES 4

SPICY FISH TAGINE
with red couscous

This recipe is for lovers of spicy food. If you prefer a milder flavour, use half the amount of chilli flakes and harissa. You can use blue-eye trevalla, snapper or any other firm white fish fillets in this recipe. Fish or chicken stock can be used instead of wine.

1 tablespoon finely grated lemon rind
2 teaspoons dried chilli flakes
2 cloves garlic, crushed
1 tablespoon olive oil
4 x 200g (6½-ounce) firm white fish fillets, skin on
30g (1 ounce) butter
2 baby fennel bulbs (260g), trimmed, cut into wedges, fronds reserved
150g (5 ounces) green beans, halved lengthways
⅓ cup (50g) raisins
1 cup (250ml) dry white wine
pinch saffron threads
⅓ cup (45g) roasted pistachios

red couscous

1 tablespoon olive oil
1 tablespoon harissa paste
2 teaspoons sweet paprika
4 green onions (scallions), sliced thinly
1 cup (250ml) chicken stock
½ cup (125ml) water
1½ cups (300g) couscous
1 tablespoon lemon juice

1 Combine rind, chilli, garlic and oil in a large bowl with fish. Cover; refrigerate for 3 hours or overnight.

2 Melt butter in a tagine (see tip) or large heavy-based frying pan over high heat; cook fennel, stirring, for 5 minutes or until browned lightly. Add beans, raisins, wine and saffron; top with fish. Bring to the boil. Reduce heat to low-medium; simmer, covered, for 15 minutes or until fish is just cooked through. Season to taste.

3 Meanwhile, make red couscous.

4 Sprinkle tagine with pistachios and reserved fennel fronds; serve with red couscous.

red couscous Heat oil in a medium saucepan over medium heat; cook harissa, paprika and half the green onion, stirring, for 2 minutes or until fragrant. Add stock and the water; bring to the boil. Remove from heat, add couscous; cover, stand 5 minutes or until liquid is absorbed. Using a fork, fluff couscous, then stir in juice; season to taste. Top with remaining green onion.

PREP + COOK TIME 35 MINUTES SERVES 4

mussel CHOWDER

Chowder is a type of soup or stew that is prepared with either milk or cream, and usually contains vegetables or seafood. Fish, corn, and clam chowders are especially popular in North America and Canada.

4 corn cobs (700g), trimmed, cleaned
2 tablespoons olive oil
100g (3 ounces) sliced prosciutto, chopped coarsely
1 medium onion (150g), chopped finely
1 clove garlic, crushed
pinch saffron threads
3 medium potatoes (600g), skin on, cut into 1cm (½-inch) pieces
1 litre (4 cups) fish stock
¼ cup (60ml) pouring cream
1kg (2 pounds) small black mussels, scrubbed, beards removed (see tips)
2 tablespoons chopped fresh chives
¼ cup coarsely chopped fresh flat-leaf parsley
crusty wholemeal or seeded bread, toasted, to serve

1 Cut kernels from corn; discard cobs. Heat oil in a large heavy-based saucepan over medium-high heat. Add prosciutto, onion, garlic and saffron; cook, stirring for 2 minutes or until onion softens. Add corn kernels, potato and stock; bring to the boil. Boil for 10 minutes or until potato is just tender.

2 Transfer 2 cups (500ml) of the soup to a blender; blend until smooth. Return to soup mixture in pan. Add cream; return to the boil. Add mussels; cook, covered, for 2 minutes, or until mussels open (see tips), stirring once. Remove from heat. Stir in chives and parsley. Serve chowder with toasted bread.

TIPS Some mussels might not open. Not all farmed mussels open up during cooking, even after excessive cooking – you do not have to discard these, just open carefully with a knife and cook a little more, if you wish. You can use vongole (clams) or pipis instead of the mussels, if you like.

PREP + COOK TIME 30 MINUTES (+ STANDING) SERVES 2

Vietnamese TURMERIC FISH

This recipe is one of Hanoi's most famous fish dishes, Cha Ca Thang Long. If using fresh turmeric, substitute 20g (¾ ounce) of fresh turmeric for every 1 teaspoon of ground turmeric. Be aware that fresh turmeric will stain your hands and plastic utensils.

300g (9½ ounces) hard tofu, cut into 3cm (1¼-inch) cubes
250g (8 ounces) dried rice vermicelli noodles
3 teaspoons ground turmeric
1 teaspoon ground white pepper
½ teaspoon sea salt flakes
¼ cup (60ml) vegetable oil
400g (12½ ounces) firm white fish fillets, cut into 2cm (¾-inch) wide strips
3 shallots (75g), sliced thinly
2 cloves garlic, crushed
1 fresh long red chilli, sliced thinly
2 tablespoons grated palm sugar
1 cup (250ml) water
¼ cup (60ml) fish sauce
⅔ cup coarsely chopped fresh dill leaves
⅓ cup (45g) roasted salted peanuts, chopped coarsely
1 lime (65g), cut into wedges

1 Place tofu on paper towel; stand for 30 minutes.

2 Meanwhile, place noodles in a medium heatproof bowl, cover with warm water; stand for 15 minutes or until just tender. Drain.

3 Combine turmeric, pepper, salt and 1 tablespoon of the oil in a medium shallow bowl; add tofu and fish, toss gently to coat.

4 Heat remaining oil in a large frying pan over medium-high heat; cook shallots, garlic and chilli until golden. Add sugar; cook, stirring, for 2 minutes or until caramelised.

5 Add the water and fish sauce; bring to the boil. Add ½ cup of the dill and the fish mixture; cook, stirring gently, until fish is just cooked through.

6 Top noodles with fish and tofu mixture, peanuts and remaining dill; serve with lime wedges.

TIP We used ling in this recipe but you can use any firm white fish you prefer, such as snapper or whiting.

PREP + COOK TIME 1 HOUR SERVES 6

prawn chu CHEE CURRY

2 cups (400g) medium-grain brown rice
1 litre (4 cups) water
½ teaspoon salt
¼ cup (60g) ghee
2½ tablespoons thai red curry paste
1kg (2 pounds) uncooked medium king prawns (shrimp), peeled, deveined, with tails intact
6 kaffir lime leaves
270ml canned coconut milk
1 cup (250ml) fish stock
2 tablespoons coconut sugar
2 tablespoons fish sauce
1 tablespoon tamarind concentrate
225g (7 ounces) canned bamboo shoots, drained, rinsed
½ cup (85g) chopped fresh pineapple
1 fresh long red chilli, seeded, shredded finely

roti bread

1 teaspoon honey
¾ cup (180ml) warm water
¼ cup (60ml) milk
⅓ cup (80ml) rice bran oil
1 egg
3 cups (450g) white spelt flour
1 teaspoon salt
60g (2 ounces) ghee

1 Make roti bread.

2 Rinse rice under cold water until water runs clear. Place rice in a medium saucepan with the water and salt; bring to the boil. Reduce heat to low; cook, covered, for 25 minutes or until water is absorbed. Remove from heat; stand, covered, for 5 minutes. Fluff with a fork and keep warm.

3 Meanwhile, heat a wok over medium-high heat. Add ghee and curry paste; cook, stirring, for 2 minutes. Add prawns and 3 crushed lime leaves; cook, stirring, for 2 minutes. Add coconut milk and stock; simmer for 5 minutes. Add sugar, sauce and tamarind. Stir in bamboo shoots and pineapple; cook for a further 2 minutes or until warmed though.

4 Finely shred remaining lime leaves; combine with chilli. Sprinkle lime leaf mixture on curry; serve with rice and warm roti bread.

roti bread Dissolve honey in a jug with the water, milk and 2 tablespoons of the oil; whisk in egg. Process flour and salt until combined. With the motor operating, gradually add milk mixture; process until it forms a sticky dough. Knead dough on a floured surface for 2 minutes or until smooth. Divide into six portions; roll into balls. Place balls in a medium bowl with remaining oil, turn to coat well. Pat a ball of dough out on a lightly oiled surface until 20cm (8-inch) round. Using oiled hands, carefully stretch dough out from the centre in a circular motion, until dough is translucent and forms a 40cm (16-inch) round (don't worry if the dough rips, this will add texture). Fold each side into the centre to form a 15cm (6-inch) square; do not press. Place on a baking-paper-lined oven tray. Repeat with remaining dough. Heat 2 teaspoons ghee in a large frying pan over medium heat; cook roti, in batches, for 2 minutes each side or until golden, adding remaining ghee with each batch.

PREP + COOK TIME 1 HOUR 30 MINUTES SERVES 4

ROSEMARY, CORN & prawn risotto

- 600g (1¼ pounds) uncooked small king prawns (shrimp)
- 1 medium onion (150g)
- 2 cloves garlic
- 2 celery stalks (300g)
- 8 x 10cm (4-inch) stalks fresh rosemary
- ½ cup (125ml) olive oil
- 3 litres (12 cups) water
- 1 cup (250ml) dry white wine
- 1½ cups (300g) arborio rice
- 2 corn cobs (500g), trimmed, cleaned
- 50g (1½ ounces) butter
- ½ cup chopped fresh flat-leaf parsley

1 Peel and devein prawns, leaving tails intact; reserve the heads and shells. Refrigerate prawns until required. Peel and finely chop onion and garlic; reserve skins. Trim celery; finely chop, reserving the trimmings. Remove rosemary leaves from the stalks; finely chop leaves, reserve stalks.

2 Heat 1 tablespoon of the oil in a large heavy-based saucepan over high heat. Add prawn heads and shells; cook, stirring, for 2 minutes. Add reserved skins and trimmings from the onion, garlic and celery, with reserved rosemary stalks. Add the water and ½ cup (125ml) of the wine; bring to the boil. Skim any scum from surface. Reduce heat to low-medium; simmer, covered, for 30 minutes. Strain stock into a heatproof bowl; discard solids. Skim any additional scum from surface. Keep warm.

3 Heat 2 tablespoons of the remaining oil in a large heavy-based saucepan over medium heat; cook chopped onion, garlic and celery, stirring, for 5 minutes or until softened. Add rice; cook, stirring, for 1 minute. Add remaining wine; cook, stirring, for 1 minute. Reduce heat to low. Add stock, one ladle at a time; cook, stirring, for 25 minutes or until stock is absorbed and rice is just cooked.

4 Meanwhile, brush corn with a little of the remaining oil; cook on a heated grill plate over high heat for 3 minutes on each side or until cooked. Remove from heat. When corn is cool enough to handle, cut kernels from cobs. Add remaining oil to reserved prawns, season; toss to combine. Cook prawns on heated grill plate for 3 minutes or until browned.

5 Add prawns and corn kernels to risotto; cook, covered, for 5 minutes or until prawns are cooked through. Stir in butter and chopped rosemary; season to taste. Serve risotto topped with parsley.

PREP + COOK TIME 40 MINUTES SERVES 4

prawn SAGANAKI

Saganaki is a popular Greek dish, named after a sagani, the two-handled frying pan in which it is cooked and served. Traditionally made with grilled or fried cheese, saganaki has evolved to include meat, vegetables and/or seafood.

1kg (2 pounds) uncooked medium king prawns (shrimp)
1 medium lemon (140g)
2 tablespoons olive oil
400g (12½ ounces) spring onions, trimmed, quartered
2 cloves garlic, chopped finely
½ cup (125ml) dry white wine
½ teaspoon caster (superfine) sugar
400g (12½ ounces) canned crushed tomatoes
4 or 5 drops Tabasco sauce
½ cup coarsely chopped fresh flat-leaf parsley
⅓ cup fresh dill sprigs
⅓ cup fresh mint leaves
180g (5½ ounces) fetta

1 Shell and devein prawns, leaving tails intact.
2 Finely grate the rind from the lemon; peel and segment lemon (see tip).
3 Heat oil in a large heavy-based frying pan over medium heat; cook spring onions and garlic, stirring, for 5 minutes or until softened. Add prawns; cook, stirring, until prawns begin to change colour. Add wine, sugar, tomatoes, sauce and half the herbs; bring to the boil over high heat. Reduce heat to a simmer.
4 Place lemon segments and crumbled fetta on top of prawns, sprinkle with rind; cook, covered, about 3 minutes or until fetta begins to melt. Season. Serve sprinkled with remaining herbs.

serving suggestion Serve with crusty bread.

TIP To segment lemon, use a small sharp knife to cut the top and bottom from lemon. Cut off the rind with the white pith, following the curve of the fruit. Holding the lemon over a bowl, cut down both sides of the white membrane to release each segment.

PREP + COOK TIME 2 HOURS SERVES 8

seafood BISQUE

A seafood bisque has a deep luxurious seafood flavour, which comes from cooking fish fillets and prawns in their shells to create a richly flavoured stock. The fish is removed and the remaining mixture is then blended (shells and all) to form a smooth, silky soup.

1.5kg (3 pounds) uncooked large king prawns (shrimp)
2 tablespoons olive oil
1 medium onion (150g), chopped coarsely
2 cloves garlic, crushed
1 medium carrot (120g), chopped
1 celery stalk (150g), chopped
6 sprigs fresh thyme
¼ cup fresh flat-leaf parsley leaves
2 tablespoons tomato paste
2 litres (8 cups) water
½ cup (125ml) dry white wine
800g (1½ pounds) firm white fish fillets, skinned
400g (12½ ounces) canned crushed tomatoes
3 medium potatoes (600g), chopped
½ cup (120g) crème fraîche
⅓ cup (80ml) lemon juice
chopped fresh flat-leaf parsley, extra, to serve

1 Shell and devein 8 prawns, keeping tails intact; place shells and heads in a large bowl. Reserve shelled prawns in a small bowl; cover; refrigerate until required.
2 Heat half the oil in a large heavy-based saucepan over high heat; cook onion, garlic, carrot and celery, stirring, for 5 minutes or until onion begins to soften. Add prawn shells and heads, with remaining unshelled prawns to pan; cook, stirring for 5 minutes or until prawns change colour. Stir in thyme, parsley and tomato paste. Add the water and wine; bring to the boil.
3 Reduce heat to low-medium, add fish; simmer for 20 minutes, skimming the surface occasionally with a ladle to remove scum. Transfer fish to a large bowl; cover until required. Increase heat to medium; add tomatoes and potatoes. Season; cook for 40 minutes or until bisque has reduced slightly. Cool for 10 minutes.
4 Blend stock mixture, in batches, until smooth. Push blended puree through a fine sieve into a clean medium saucepan over heat; return to the boil.
5 Meanwhile, heat remaining oil in a large frying pan over medium-high heat; cook reserved prawns for 1 minute on each side or until just cooked through. Flake reserved fish into bite-sized pieces.
6 Stir crème fraîche and juice into soup; season to taste. Ladle soup into bowls; top with flaked fish, prawns and chopped parsley.

PREP + COOK TIME 25 MINUTES SERVES 4

harissa & tomato PRAWNS WITH FETTA

Harissa is a North African paste made from dried red chillies, garlic, olive oil and caraway seeds. It is available from Middle Eastern food shops and supermarkets.

- 1 tablespoon olive oil
- 1 medium onion (150g), sliced thinly
- 2 cloves garlic, sliced thinly
- ¼ cup (60ml) dry white wine
- 20 uncooked banana prawns (shrimp) (700g), shelled, deveined, with tails intact
- 2 teaspoons harissa paste
- 400g (12½ ounces) canned diced tomatoes
- 2 tablespoons currants
- 1 teaspoon caster (superfine) sugar
- 2 cups (400g) whole wheat couscous
- 2 cups (500ml) boiling water
- 100g (3 ounces) greek fetta, crumbled
- 2 teaspoons olive oil, extra
- 2 tablespoons fresh flat-leaf parsley leaves

1 Preheat a grill (broiler) to high.

2 Heat oil in a large, deep ovenproof frying pan over medium heat; cook onion and garlic for 5 minutes or until soft. Add wine; cook over high heat for 30 seconds. Add prawns and harissa; cook, stirring occasionally, for 2 minutes. Add tomatoes, currants and sugar. Reduce heat to low; cook for 3 minutes or until prawns are just cooked. Season.

3 Meanwhile, place couscous and the boiling water in a large bowl. Cover with plastic wrap; stand for 5 minutes or until water is absorbed. Fluff couscous with a fork; season to taste.

4 Top prawns with fetta; drizzle with extra oil. Place pan under grill for 2 minutes or until fetta is golden. Sprinkle prawns with parsley; serve with couscous.

TIPS If you don't like things too spicy, replace 1 teaspoon of harissa with 1 teaspoon cumin seeds.
If you don't have an ovenproof frying pan, wrap the handle of your pan in several layers of foil.

smoky brazil nuts & almonds

sesame & seaweed sprinkle

quinoa crisp

almond gremolata

soup & salad seeds

parmesan crisps

Toppers

Bulk up a soup or stew, while adding a textural layer, with a choice of one of these six toppers.

SMOKY BRAZIL NUTS & ALMONDS

PREP + COOK TIME 20 MINUTES MAKES 1 CUP

Preheat oven to 180°C/350°F. Line an oven tray with baking paper. Coarsely chop 1 cup brazil nuts; place on tray with 1 cup blanched almonds and 1 cup rice puffs. Whisk 1 egg white, 2 teaspoons smoked paprika, 1 teaspoon ground cumin and 1 teaspoon sea salt flakes with a fork until combined. Toss spice mixture with nut mixture. Roast for 10 minutes or until golden, stirring halfway through cooking time.

SESAME & SEAWEED SPRINKLE

PREP + COOK TIME 15 MINUTES MAKES 1¼ CUPS

Using scissors snip 2 nori (seaweed) sheets into fine strips. Place ¼ cup sesame seeds and 1 teaspoon sea salt flakes in a small frying pan; stir constantly over medium heat for 5 minutes or until golden. Add nori strips and stir a further 1 minute or until lightly toasted. Transfer to a bowl; stir in ¼ cup fried asian shallots and 1 teaspoon dried chilli flakes.

QUINOA CRISP

PREP + COOK TIME 1 HOUR 30 MINUTES MAKES 2 CUPS

Preheat oven to 180°C/350°F. Line an oven tray with baking paper. Combine ⅓ cup white quinoa, 2 tablespoons black chia seeds, 2 tablespoons linseeds (flaxseeds), 1 tablespoon extra virgin olive oil and 1 cup water in a small saucepan. Stir over medium heat for 12 minutes until mixture begins to pull away from side of pan and is thick. Add ⅓ cup finely grated parmesan; stir a further 2 minutes. Remove from heat; season. Spread mixture thinly over tray. Cover with a second sheet of baking paper; roll out to 2mm (⅛-in) thick. Bake for 20 minutes; remove top paper. Bake a further 20 minutes. Carefully turn crisp over; bake for 20 minutes or until golden brown and crisp. Cool. Break into pieces.

ALMOND GREMOLATA

PREP + COOK TIME 10 MINUTES MAKES 1 CUP

Coarsely chop ½ cup roasted natural almonds. Heat 30g (1oz) butter in a small saucepan over a medium heat; cook, stirring, until beginning to brown; remove from heat. Add 1 tablespoon finely grated lemon rind and ½ cup chopped fresh flat-leaf parsley.

SOUP & SALAD SEEDS

PREP + COOK TIME 10 MINUTES MAKES ¾ CUP

Heat 2 tablespoons olive oil in a small, non-stick frying pan over medium heat. Add ⅓ cup coarsely chopped natural almonds and ¼ cup pepitas (pumpkin seed kernels), cook, stirring, for 1 minute. Add 1 tablespoon each of coriander and black sesame seeds; cook, stirring, for a further 2 minutes or until lightly toasted. Cool to room temperature.

PARMESAN CRISPS

PREP + COOK TIME 20 MINUTES MAKES 6

Preheat oven to 180°C/350°F. Line two oven trays with baking paper. Combine 1 cup finely grated parmesan, 2 teaspoons wholemeal plain (all-purpose) flour, ¼ teaspoon freshly ground black pepper and 1 teaspoon finely chopped fresh rosemary leaves in a medium bowl. Place 12 level tablespoons of mixture onto tray, 5cm (2in) apart; flatten to 8cm (3¼-in) rounds. Bake for 6 minutes or until pale golden. Working quickly, lift using a palette knife; drape over a rolling pin to cool.

PREP + COOK TIME 55 MINUTES (+ COOLING) SERVES 6

fisherman's CASSEROLE

This is the seafood's lover's dream dinner, packed full of fresh mussels, prawns and salmon; use whatever seafood is fresh and plentiful at your local fishmonger. You could also use marinara mix, if you prefer.

⅓ cup (80ml) olive oil
750g (1½ pounds) cauliflower, cut into 3cm (1¼-inch) florets
1 large fennel bulb (550g), halved, sliced, fronds reserved
600g (1¼ pounds) crème fraîche
2 tablespoons plain (all-purpose) flour
½ cup fresh dill, chopped
½ teaspoon ground nutmeg
1 teaspoon finely grated lemon rind, plus 1 teaspoon extra to serve
1kg (2 pounds) small black mussels, scrubbed, beards removed
250g (8 ounces) uncooked prawns (shrimp), shelled, deveined
500g (1 pound) skinless boneless salmon fillet, cut into 3cm (1¼-inch) pieces

1 Heat 2 tablespoons of the oil in large frying pan over medium-high heat. Add cauliflower; cook, stirring, for 10 minutes or until starting to brown. Transfer to a plate.

2 Heat remaining oil in same pan. Add fennel; cook, stirring for 10 minutes or until just tender.

3 Meanwhile, combine crème fraîche, flour, dill, nutmeg and rind in a medium bowl; season.

4 Preheat oven to 200°C/400°F.

5 Heat a large heavy-based saucepan over high heat. Add mussels; cook, covered, shaking pan occasionally, for 2 minutes or until mussels just open. Drain mussels. Remove mussels from shells; cool.

6 Add mussels, prawns and salmon to crème fraîche mixture. Transfer mixture to a 3 litre (12-cup) ovenproof dish; top with cauliflower and fennel.

7 Bake for 25 minutes or until top is golden and seafood is cooked. Serve sprinkled with reserved fennel fronds and extra lemon rind.

serving suggestion Serve with crusty bread.

PREP + COOK TIME 25 MINUTES SERVES 4

Thai green PRAWN CURRY

As this is a Thai curry based on coconut milk and fresh green chillies, the color comes out creamy mild green or, as this colour is called in Thai, 'sweet green'. You could add other vegetables to the curry, such as eggplant, capsicum or potato, if you like.

24 uncooked medium king prawns (shrimp) (1kg)
1 tablespoon vegetable oil
¼ cup (75g) thai green curry paste
4 kaffir lime leaves
10cm (4-inch) stalk fresh lemon grass (20g), cut into three pieces
2 cups (500ml) coconut milk
¾ cup (180ml) water
1½ tablespoons fish sauce
150g (4½ ounces) snake beans, cut into 4cm (1½-inch) pieces
⅓ cup (50g) fresh or frozen peas
2 teaspoons grated palm sugar
½ cup fresh thai basil leaves
2 limes (130g), cut into wedges

1 Shell and devein prawns, leaving tails intact. Butterfly prawns by cutting along the centre back without cutting all the way through.

2 Heat oil in a large frying pan over medium heat; cook paste, lime leaves and lemon grass, stirring for 3 minutes or until fragrant. Add coconut milk, the water, fish sauce, beans and peas; simmer, stirring, for 3 minutes or until beans and peas are almost tender.

3 Add prawns; cook for 1 minute or until prawns are just cooked through. Stir in sugar. Season to taste with extra fish sauce or sugar, if needed.

4 Top curry with thai basil; serve with lime wedges.

serving suggestion Serve with steamed jasmine rice.

PREP + COOK TIME 1 HOUR 45 MINUTES SERVES 10

Sri lankan SEAFOOD CURRY

1.75kg (3½ pounds) firm white fish fillets
1kg (2 pounds) uncooked large king prawns (shrimp)
3 fresh long green chillies
2 large onions (600g), chopped coarsely
6 cloves garlic, chopped coarsely
4cm (1½-inch) piece fresh ginger (20g), chopped coarsely
2 tablespoons olive oil
1 tablespoon ground cumin
3 teaspoons ground turmeric
¼ cup fresh curry leaves
750g (1½ pounds) ripe tomatoes, chopped
1½ cups (375ml) chicken or fish stock
2 cups (500ml) coconut cream
1 tablespoon fish sauce
1½ teaspoons caster (superfine) sugar

tomato sambal

3 medium ripe tomatoes (450g), cut into 1cm (½-inch) pieces
1 small red onion (100g), chopped finely
1 fresh long green chilli, seeded, chopped finely
2 teaspoons tamarind concentrate
1 teaspoon brown sugar
2 tablespoons fresh coriander (cilantro) leaves
½ cup (25g) coconut flakes, toasted

coconut rice

800ml canned coconut milk
2⅔ cups (680ml) water
4 cups (800g) basmati rice

1 Cut fish into 6cm (2½-inch) pieces. Shell and devein prawns, leaving tails intact. Cover seafood, separately; refrigerate until required.

2 Remove seeds from half the chillies, then chop all chillies coarsely. Process chilli, onion, garlic and ginger until chopped finely.

3 Heat oil in a large heavy-based saucepan over medium heat; cook onion mixture, stirring, for 7 minutes or until softened. Reduce heat to low, add cumin, turmeric and curry leaves; cook, stirring, for 5 minutes. Increase heat to high, add tomatoes and stock; bring to the boil. Reduce heat; simmer for 15 minutes. Add coconut cream; simmer for a further 10 minutes or until vegetables are tender and flavours are developed. Add fish sauce and sugar; season.

4 Meanwhile, make tomato sambal and coconut rice.

5 Add fish to curry sauce; simmer for 2 minutes. Add prawns; simmer for a further 3 minutes or until prawns and fish are just cooked through.

6 Top curry with extra curry leaves; serve with tomato sambal and coconut rice.

tomato sambal Combine all ingredients except coconut in a medium bowl. Season. Cover; refrigerate until required. Just before serving, stir in coconut.

coconut rice Bring coconut milk and the water to the boil in a large saucepan over medium heat. Add rice, return just to the boil, then cover with a tight-fitting lid. Reduce heat to lowest setting; cook for 16 minutes or until rice is tender and liquid absorbed. Remove from heat; stand, covered, for 10 minutes. Fluff rice with a fork.

TIPS You will need thick skinless, boneless fish fillets, such as blue-eye trevalla, ling or snapper. Curry sauce can be made to the end of step 3, up to 2 days ahead; cover and refrigerate.

PREP + COOK TIME 45 MINUTES SERVES 4

fish & fennel STEW

Tomatoes are acidic, so balancing out their flavour with a sweetener such as panera sugar or another unrefined sugar is helpful. We used snapper here. You could add extra seafood to the stew, such as uncooked prawns and mussels.

¼ cup (60ml) extra virgin olive oil
1 medium onion (150g), chopped finely
2 medium fennel bulbs (600g), fronds reserved, sliced thinly
2 cloves garlic, crushed
1 fresh long red chilli, sliced thinly
½ cup (125ml) dry white wine
3 cups (750ml) fish stock
800g (1½ pounds) canned diced tomatoes
¼ teaspoon unrefined sugar (see above), optional
750g (1½ pounds) firm white fish fillets, cut into 3cm (1¼-inch) pieces
2 tablespoons coarsely chopped fresh flat-leaf parsley leaves
4 slices seeded sourdough bread (280g)
2 teaspoons finely grated lemon rind
1 medium lemon (140g), cut into cheeks

1 Heat 1½ tablespoons of the oil in a large saucepan over medium heat. Add onion and fennel; cook, stirring, for 5 minutes or until softened. Add garlic and chilli; cook for 1 minute or until fragrant.
2 Add wine; bring to the boil. Add stock, tomatoes and sugar; bring to the boil. Reduce heat to low-medium; cook, covered, for 20 minutes. Season. Add fish; cook, covered, stirring occasionally, for a further 5 minutes or until fish is cooked through. Stir in parsley.
3 Just before serving, heat a grill pan (or plate) over medium heat. Brush bread with remaining oil; cook for 1 minute each side or until golden and lightly charred.
4 Top stew with lemon rind and reserved fennel fronds. Serve with grilled sourdough and lemon cheeks.

VEGETARIAN

PREP + COOK TIME 35 MINUTES SERVES 4

chickpea & PINE NUT STEW

Chickpeas are an often overlooked legume, full of protein, fibre and folate. They can be eaten cold in salads, ground into flour, fried as falafel, baked into a flatbread, used in stews (as in this recipe), or blended to make hummus.

1 tablespoon olive oil
1 medium onion (150g), chopped finely
2 cloves garlic, crushed
1 fresh long red chilli, chopped finely
400g (12½ ounces) canned diced tomatoes
1 cup (280g) tomato passata
285g (9 ounces) bottled piquillo peppers, drained, chopped coarsely
1 cup (250ml) vegetable stock or water
¼ teaspoon saffron threads
800g (1 ½ pounds) canned chickpeas (garbanzo beans), drained, rinsed
1½ tablespoons pine nuts, toasted
¼ cup (30g) finely grated manchego cheese (see tip)
¼ cup fresh flat-leaf parsley leaves

1 Heat oil in a large heavy-based saucepan over medium-high heat; cook onion, stirring, for 5 minutes or until onion softens. Add garlic and chilli; cook, stirring, for 1 minute or until fragrant.

2 Add tomatoes, passata, peppers, stock, saffron and chickpeas; bring to the boil. Reduce heat to low-medium; simmer for 15 minutes or until reduced slightly. Season to taste.

3 Serve topped with pine nuts, cheese and parsley.

serving suggestion Serve with toasted multigrain sourdough bread.

TIP Manchego cheese is a semi-firm Spanish sheep's milk cheese available from selected supermarkets or delis. You can use parmesan or pecorino cheese instead, if you like.

PREP + COOK TIME 1 HOUR 50 MINUTES (+ STANDING) SERVES 4

vegetable CASSOULET

Cassoulet is a slow-cooked French casserole, traditionally containing meat (typically pork sausages, goose, duck or mutton), pork skin (couennes) and white beans (haricots blancs). This is our vegetarian version, topped with crisp herby bread.

2 teaspoons olive oil
4 shallots (100g), halved
3 cloves garlic, sliced thinly
2 medium carrots (240g), chopped coarsely
200g (6½ ounces) swiss brown mushrooms, halved
1 cup (250ml) dry white wine
2 medium zucchini (240g), chopped coarsely
1½ cups (375ml) vegetable stock
700g (1½ pounds) tomato passata
1 teaspoon finely chopped fresh thyme leaves
400g (12½ ounces) canned borlotti beans, drained, rinsed

bread topping

1 tablespoon olive oil
1 small onion (80g), chopped finely
1 clove garlic, crushed
2 teaspoons finely grated lemon rind
2 teaspoons finely chopped fresh thyme leaves
½ wholegrain and seed sourdough loaf (220g), torn into 2cm (¾-inch) pieces
2 tablespoons coarsely chopped fresh flat-leaf parsley

1 Preheat oven to 180°C/350°F.

2 Heat oil in a large flameproof casserole dish over medium-high heat; cook shallots, garlic, carrot and mushrooms, stirring, for 5 minutes or until vegetables are just tender. Add wine; bring to the boil. Boil until liquid is reduced by half. Add zucchini, stock, passata, thyme and beans; return to the boil. Remove from heat. Transfer to oven; cook, covered, for 50 minutes.

3 Meanwhile, make bread topping.

4 Season cassoulet to taste, sprinkle with bread topping; return to oven, cook, uncovered, for 10 minutes or until bread topping is browned.

bread topping Heat olive oil in a large frying pan over medium-high heat; cook onion, stirring, for 5 minutes or until soft. Add garlic, rind, thyme and bread; cook, stirring, for 10 minutes or until bread browns lightly. Stir in parsley.

serving suggestion Serve with a bitter leaf salad.

PREP + COOK TIME 1 HOUR SERVES 4

CHILLI BEANS *with chimichurri*

2 chipotle chillies
½ cup (125ml) boiling water
1 tablespoon olive oil
1 large onion (200g), chopped finely
2 teaspoons ground cumin
2 teaspoons ground coriander
1 teaspoon mexican chilli powder
400g (12½ ounces) canned red kidney beans, drained, rinsed
400g (12½ ounces) canned chickpeas (garbanzo beans), drained, rinsed
2 x 400g (12½ ounces) canned diced tomatoes
¼ cup (60ml) water
½ cup fresh coriander (cilantro) sprigs
¼ cup (60g) sour cream

tortilla crisps

4 x 17cm (6¾ inch) white corn tortillas, quartered
cooking-oil spray
½ teaspoon sweet paprika

chimichurri

½ small red onion (50g), chopped finely
1 clove garlic, chopped finely
½ teaspoon sweet paprika
½ cup (125ml) olive oil
1½ tablespoons red wine vinegar
½ cup finely chopped fresh flat-leaf parsley
2 tablespoons finely chopped fresh oregano

1 Place chipotle chillies in a small heatproof bowl, cover with the boiling water; stand for 20 minutes. Drain; reserve soaking liquid. Coarsely chop chillies; discard stems. Blend or process chopped chillies with soaking liquid until smooth.

2 Meanwhile, make tortilla crisps then chimichurri.

3 Heat oil in a large saucepan over medium heat; cook onion, stirring, for 5 minutes or until onion softens. Add cumin, ground coriander and chilli powder; cook, stirring, for 1 minute or until fragrant.

4 Add beans, chickpeas, chipotle mixture, tomatoes and the water; bring to the boil. Reduce heat; cook for 15 minutes or until sauce thickens.

5 Top chilli beans with chimichurri and fresh coriander; serve with tortilla crisps and sour cream.

tortilla crisps Preheat oven to 200°C/400°F. Spray tortillas with oil; sprinkle with paprika. Place on an oven tray; bake for 5 minutes or until crisp.

chimichurri Combine ingredients in a small bowl; season.

serving suggestion Serve with guacamole and lime wedges.

PREP + COOK TIME 45 MINUTES SERVES 6

pumpkin, eggplant & CHICKPEA CURRY

This is a super simple vegetable curry that will be on the table in less than an hour. You could use a variety of vegetables instead of the eggplant and pumpkin, if you like, such as orange sweet potato, carrot, cauliflower or other root vegetables.

2 tablespoons vegetable oil
1 medium onion (150g), sliced thickly
1 clove garlic, crushed
2cm (¾-inch) piece fresh ginger (10g), grated finely
2 fresh small red thai (serrano) chillies, chopped finely
1 teaspoon ground cumin
½ teaspoon ground turmeric
¼ teaspoon ground cardamom
¼ teaspoon ground fennel
8 baby eggplants (480g), sliced thickly
1kg (2 pounds) butternut pumpkin, cut into 1cm (½-inch) slices
400g (12½ ounces) canned diced tomatoes
400ml canned coconut cream
1 cup (250ml) vegetable stock
1 tablespoon tomato paste
400g (12½ ounces) canned chickpeas (garbanzo beans), drained, rinsed
½ cup fresh mint leaves

1 Heat oil in a large heavy-based saucepan over medium-high heat; cook onion, garlic, ginger and chilli, stirring, for 5 minutes or until onion softens. Add spices and eggplant; cook, stirring, for 2 minutes.
2 Add pumpkin, tomatoes, coconut cream, stock and tomato paste; bring to the boil. Reduce heat to low-medium; cook for 20 minutes. Add chickpeas; simmer for a further 10 minutes or until vegetables are tender. Season to taste.
3 Serve curry topped with mint leaves.

serving suggestion Serve with steamed jasmine rice.

PREP + COOK TIME 30 MINUTES SERVES 4

potato & egg RENDANG

Rendang curry originated in Indonesia, where it is commonly a meat dish, comprising of either beef, lamb or goat. This vegetarian version uses potato to bulk up the curry sauce, and is topped with a crisp fried egg,

8 small potatoes (750g), chopped coarsely
¼ cup (60ml) vegetable oil
1 medium onion (150g), chopped finely
185g (6 ounces) rendang curry paste
270ml canned coconut milk
⅓ cup (80ml) water
4 eggs
1 cup fresh coriander (cilantro) leaves

1 Boil, steam or microwave potatoes until just tender; drain.

2 Meanwhile, heat 2 tablespoons of the oil in a medium heavy-based saucepan over medium heat; cook onion and curry paste, stirring, for 3 minutes or until onion is softened and paste is fragrant.

3 Stir in coconut milk and the water; bring to a simmer. Add potato; cook for 5 minutes, stirring occasionally. Press potatoes lightly to crush slightly. Season to taste.

4 Heat remaining oil in a large frying pan over medium-high heat. Break eggs into pan; cook eggs until the edges are crisp, whites are firm and the yolks are cooked to your liking

5 Divide curry between serving bowls; top with fried eggs and coriander.

serving suggestion Serve with steamed rice or roti and lime wedges.

PREP + COOK TIME 45 MINUTES SERVES 4

Sri lankan potato & pea curry WITH FRIED EGGS

Curry powders are a blend of ground spices used for making Indian and some South-East Asian dishes. They usally consist of the following spices: dried chilli, cinnamon, coriander, cumin, fennel, cardamom and turmeric. We used dutch cream potatoes in this recipe.

4 medium potatoes (800g), chopped coarsely
¼ cup (60g) ghee
1 medium onion (150g), sliced thinly
4 cloves garlic, chopped finely
2½ tablespoons finely chopped fresh ginger
2 sprigs fresh curry leaves
1 tablespoon curry powder
1½ teaspoons brown mustard seeds
½ teaspoon ground turmeric
2 fresh long green chillies, sliced thinly
400g (12½ ounces) canned chickpeas (garbanzo beans), drained, rinsed
1 cup (120g) frozen peas
½ cup (125ml) water
½ teaspoon finely grated lime rind
1 tablespoon lime juice
4 eggs
2 green onions (scallions), sliced thinly
1 cup fresh coriander (cilantro) leaves

1 Place potatoes in a large saucepan with enough cold water to just cover; bring to the boil. Boil over medium heat for 15 minutes or until tender; drain.

2 Heat 2 tablespoons of the ghee in a large heavy-based frying pan over medium heat; cook onion, stirring, for 5 minutes or until softened. Add garlic, ginger, curry leaves, curry powder, seeds, turmeric and half the chilli; cook, stirring, for 1 minute or until fragrant.

3 Add potatoes, chickpeas, peas and the water; bring to the boil. Reduce heat to medium; simmer, for 3 minutes or until peas are tender. Stir in rind and juice; season to taste.

4 Heat remaining ghee in a large frying pan over medium-high heat; cook eggs for 2 minutes or until the whites are set and yolks are cooked to your liking.

5 Serve curry topped with fried egg, green onion, coriander and remaining chilli.

PREP + COOK TIME 30 MINUTES SERVES 4

chickpea SHAKSHOUKA

Shakshouka, a trendy cafe food commonly served at breakfast, comes from an Arabic slang word meaning 'a mixture'. It refers to the sauce in the dish, usually a mix of tomatoes, chilli and onions, in which the eggs are cooked.

1 teaspoon caraway seeds
1 teaspoon cumin seeds
1 teaspoon smoked paprika
2 tablespoons olive oil
2 cloves garlic, crushed
1 fresh long red chilli, chopped finely
1 large onion (200g), chopped coarsely
1 large red capsicum (bell pepper) (350g), chopped coarsely
400g (12½ ounces) canned chickpeas (garbanzo beans), drained, rinsed
400g (12½ ounces) canned diced tomatoes
1 cup (250ml) water
2 teaspoons harissa paste
2 teaspoons caster (superfine) sugar
4 eggs
¼ cup fresh coriander (cilantro) leaves

1 Heat a large deep ovenproof frying pan over medium heat; cook seeds and paprika, stirring, for 1 minute. Add oil, garlic and chilli; cook for 1 minute or until fragrant.

2 Add onion and capsicum; cook, stirring, for 8 minutes or until onion is softened. Add chickpeas, tomatoes, the water, harissa and sugar; bring to the boil. Reduce heat to medium; simmer for 5 minutes or until vegetables are tender and liquid has thickened slightly.

3 Using a spoon, make four shallow indents in the tomato mixture. Crack 1 egg into each hole. Cook, covered, over low heat, for 5 minutes or until whites are set and yolks are still runny, or until cooked to your liking. Serve topped with coriander.

TIP Harissa is a hot paste; there are many different brands available on the market, and the strengths can vary enormously. If you have a low heat-level tolerance, you may find this, and any other recipe containing harissa, too hot to tolerate, even if you reduce the amount.

PREP + COOK TIME 1 HOUR SERVES 4

root vegetable TAGINE

Ras el hanout is a Moroccan spice blend which can be found at some supermarkets and specialty food stores. Literally translating to 'top of the shop', it can include up to 12 different spices, and is used in many savoury dishes, and rubbed on meat or fish.

¼ cup (60ml) olive oil
2 small parsnips (240g), quartered lengthways
2 small carrots (140g), quartered lengthways
1 small orange sweet potato (250g), quartered lengthways
1 medium onion (150g), chopped coarsely
4 cloves garlic, sliced thinly
1½ tablespoons ras el hanout
800g (1½ pounds) canned diced tomatoes
400g (12½ ounces) canned chickpeas (garbanzo beans), drained, rinsed
1 cup (170g) pitted prunes
1½ cups (375ml) vegetable stock
2 cups (400g) couscous
2 cups (500ml) boiling water
1 cup (280g) Greek-style yoghurt
2 teaspoons harissa paste
2 tablespoons thinly sliced preserved lemon rind (see tip)
¼ cup (40g) pomegranate seeds
½ cup loosely packed fresh mint leaves

1 Heat oil in a large heavy-based saucepan over medium heat; cook parsnip, carrot, sweet potato, onion, garlic and ras el hanout, stirring occasionally, for 10 minutes or until tender.

2 Add tomatoes, chickpeas, prunes and stock; bring to the boil. Reduce heat to low; simmer, covered, for 40 minutes or until vegetables are tender. Season.

3 Meanwhile, combine couscous and the water in a large heatproof bowl, cover; stand for 5 minutes or until liquid is absorbed, fluffing with a fork occasionally.

4 Place yoghurt in a small bowl; swirl harissa through.

5 Top tagine with preserved lemon, pomegranate seeds and mint; serve with couscous and yoghurt mixture.

TIP Preserved lemon is available at delicatessens and some supermarkets. Remove and discard the flesh, rinse the rind well, then slice thinly. You will need about 2 preserved lemon wedges (70g) for this recipe.

PREP + COOK TIME 30 MINUTES SERVES 2

cauliflower & tofu RED CURRY

We used canned coconut milk that hasn't been emulsified, so it separates with the solid rising to the surface. If you have coconut milk that is emulsified, skip the step of adding the solids first.

1 tablespoon peanut oil
1 medium onion (150g), sliced thinly
400ml canned coconut milk (do not shake can) (see above)
⅓ cup (100g) red curry paste
2 teaspoons soy sauce
1 tablespoon lime juice
1 tablespoon brown sugar
¾ cup (180ml) water
400g (12½ ounces) cauliflower, sliced thickly
250g (8 ounces) green beans, trimmed, halved lengthways
1 large zucchini (150g), sliced thickly
110g (3½ ounces) tofu puffs, cut in half diagonally
⅓ cup (25g) shaved fresh coconut (see tips), toasted lightly
⅓ cup loosely packed fresh coriander (cilantro) leaves
1 fresh long red chilli, sliced thinly
lime wedges, to serve

1 Heat oil in a wok over medium heat; stir-fry onion, for 2 minutes or until softened.

2 Add a spoonful of the solid coconut milk from the top of the can to wok. Add curry paste; cook, stirring, for 3 minutes or until oil separates and rises to the surface. Stir in soy sauce, lime juice, sugar, remaining coconut milk and the water; bring to the boil. Reduce heat to low-medium, add cauliflower; simmer, covered, for 5 minutes. Add beans and zucchini; simmer, partially covered, for 5 minutes or until vegetables are tender. Add tofu; stir until hot.

3 Serve curry immediately topped with shaved coconut, coriander and chilli and lime wedges.

serving suggestion Serve curry with steamed jasmine rice.

TIPS To shave flesh from a fresh coconut, wrap the coconut in an old, clean tea towel and firmly hit the coconut on a hard floor, ideally outside and close to a bowl to catch the coconut water. Separate and discard the hard outer shell of the coconut. Use a vegetable peeler to shave the flesh. If fresh coconut is not available, use moist coconut flakes instead. Serve curry immediately, as tofu will continue to absorb liquid on standing.

PREP + COOK TIME 2 HOURS (+ COOLING) SERVES 6

POTATO & MUSHROOM CASSEROLE
with crunchy potato topping

50g (1½ ounces) butter
1 large onion (200g), chopped finely
2 cloves garlic, crushed
1kg (2 pounds) mixed mushrooms, sliced
½ cup (125ml) dry white wine
1 cup (125g) finely grated gruyère cheese
1 cup (80g) finely grated parmesan
1 tablespoon finely chopped fresh rosemary leaves
1kg (2 pounds) small desiree potatoes, unpeeled, cut into 5mm (¼-inch) slices
⅓ cup (80ml) milk
300ml thickened (heavy) cream
1 tablespoon fresh rosemary sprigs, extra

1 Preheat oven to 180°C/350°F. Grease three 1-litre (4-cup) ovenproof dishes.

2 Melt butter in a large heavy-based saucepan over medium heat; cook onion and garlic, stirring, for 5 minutes, or until onion is soft but not browned. Add half the mushrooms; cook, stirring occasionally, for 5 minutes. Add remaining mushrooms; cook, stirring occasionally, for 8 minutes or until mushrooms have released their juices and most of the liquid has evaporated. Stir in wine; bring to the boil. Reduce heat; simmer until liquid is reduced by half. Remove from heat; season to taste.

3 Combine cheeses and chopped rosemary in a small bowl. Cover base of the dishes with slightly-overlapping potato slices. Sprinkle with one-third of the cheese mixture, then half the mushroom mixture. Repeat with another layer of potato and remaining mushroom mixture. Arrange remaining potato slices, slightly overlapping, around the edge of the dishes. Stir milk and cream together; pour over potato layers. Refrigerate remaining cheese mixture.

4 Cover dishes loosely with foil. Bake for 1 hour or until bubbling. Remove foil; sprinkle remaining cheese mixture over potato. Bake for 30 minutes or until potato is tender and top is golden. Stand for 15 minutes before serving. Serve topped with extra rosemary.

TIPS We used a combination of king brown, swiss brown and button mushrooms; you can use any combination of mushrooms you prefer. Use a mandoline or V-slicer to cut the potatoes into very thin slices.

PREP + COOK TIME 45 MINUTES SERVES 4

VEGETARIAN CHILLI *with guacamole*

Chocolate might seem like an odd choice to add to a savoury dish, but the inclusion of dark chocolate adds body, colour and flavour to this vegetarian chilli. Use a good quality chocolate, with 70% cocoa solids, so as to not make the chilli too sweet.

2 celery stalks (300g)
2 tablespoons olive oil
1 large onion (200g), chopped coarsely
1 medium yellow capsicum (bell pepper) (200g), chopped coarsely
1 large red capsicum (bell pepper) (350g), chopped coarsely
2 fresh long red chillies, chopped finely
1 tablespoon smoked paprika
3 cloves garlic, crushed
2 teaspoons ground coriander
2 teaspoons fresh oregano leaves
2 cups (500ml) vegetable stock
400g (12½ ounces) canned diced tomatoes
40g (1½ ounces) dark chocolate (70% cocoa), grated
400g (12½ ounces) canned four-bean mix, drained, rinsed
1 tablespoon unrefined sugar (see tips)
¾ cup (90g) finely grated vintage cheddar
1 packet (156g) blue corn chips

guacamole
2 medium avocados (500g)
juice of 1 large lime (100g)

1 Make guacamole.

2 Wash celery stalks well, remove leafy tips and reserve. Chop celery into 1cm (½-inch) pieces. Heat oil in a large saucepan over medium heat; cook celery, onion and capsicum, stirring, for 5 minutes or until softened. Add chilli, paprika, garlic, coriander and oregano; cook, stirring, for 1 minute or until fragrant. Add stock and tomatoes; bring to a simmer. Simmer, stirring occasionally, for 10 minutes or until thickened. Add chocolate, beans and sugar; cook, stirring, for 5 minutes or until dark and glossy. Season to taste.

3 Top chilli with cheddar and reserved celery leaves; serve with guacamole and corn chips.

guacamole Halve avocados; remove seeds. Place avocado flesh in a medium bowl with juice; season to taste. Mash with a fork until smooth. Cover; refrigerate until required.

TIPS We used panela sugar, also known as rapadura, but any unrefined whole cane sugar can be used. Use yellow corn chips or tortilla chips, if you can't find blue corn chips.

PREP + COOK TIME 3 HOURS 15 MINUTES SERVES 4

QUINOA, BLACK BEAN & chipotle chilli

You will need a slow cooker for this recipe.

½ cup (100g) tri-colour quinoa
1 tablespoon olive oil
1 medium onion (150g), chopped finely
1 medium red capsicum (bell pepper) (200g), chopped finely
1 medium green capsicum (bell pepper) (200g), chopped finely
3 cloves garlic, crushed
2 teaspoons ground cumin
2 teaspoons dried oregano
½ teaspoon mexican chilli powder
375g (12 ounces) bottled chipotle thick and chunky salsa
2½ cups (625ml) vegetable stock
800g (1½-pounds) canned black beans, drained, rinsed
2 trimmed corn cobs (500g), kernels removed
½ cup fresh coriander (cilantro) sprigs

1 Rinse quinoa well; drain.

2 Heat oil in a 4.5-litre (18-cup) slow cooker on sear (HIGH) setting; cook onion, capsicum and garlic, stirring, for 5 minutes or until vegetables soften. Add cumin, oregano and chilli; cook, stirring, for 1 minute or until fragrant.

3 Add quinoa, salsa, stock and beans; stir to combine. Cook, covered, on low setting, for 2½ hours.

4 Add corn kernels to cooker; cook, covered, on high, for 30 minutes or until corn is tender. Season to taste.

5 Serve chilli topped with coriander.

serving suggestion Serve with guacamole, corn chips, sour cream and lime cheeks.

PREP + COOK TIME 2 HOURS 30 MINUTES SERVES 4

Indian-style LENTIL STEW

You will need a slow cooker for this recipe.

1 tablespoon olive oil
1 medium onion (150g), chopped finely
3 cloves garlic, crushed
1 tablespoon black mustard seeds
1 tablespoon ground coriander
2 teaspoons ground cumin
1 teaspoon ground turmeric
½ teaspoon dried chilli flakes
1 cinnamon stick
1½ cups (300g) green lentils
2½ cups (625ml) vegetable stock
1 cup (250ml) canned coconut cream
150g (4½ ounces) baby spinach leaves
½ cup (120g) Greek-style yoghurt
2 tablespoons micro herbs, optional

1 Heat oil in a 4.5-litre (18-cup) slow cooker on sear (HIGH) setting; cook onion and garlic, stirring, for 5 minutes or until softened.
2 Add mustard seeds, coriander, cumin, turmeric, chilli and cinnamon to cooker; cook, stirring, for 1 minute or until fragrant.
3 Add lentils, stock and coconut cream; stir to combine. Cook, covered, on low setting for 2 hours.
4 Discard cinnamon. Stir in spinach; season to taste. Serve topped with yoghurt and micro herbs.

serving suggestion Serve with cauliflower rice (see page 126) and grilled roti bread.

PREP + COOK TIME 4 HOURS 30 MINUTES SERVES 4

mixed bean, spinach & PANEER ROGAN JOSH

You will need a slow cooker for this recipe.

½ cup (150g) rogan josh curry paste
2 large onions (400g), sliced thinly
2 teaspoons finely grated fresh ginger
3 cloves garlic, crushed
400g (12½ ounces) canned diced tomatoes
840g (1¾ pounds) canned four-bean mix, drained, rinsed
2 dried bay leaves
2 cups (500ml) vegetable stock
150g (4½ ounces) baby spinach leaves
200g (6½ ounces) paneer, crumbled
micro herbs, to serve, optional

1 Heat a 4.5-litre (18-cup) slow cooker on sauté (MEDIUM) setting; cook curry paste, stirring, for 5 minutes or until fragrant. Add onion, ginger, garlic, tomatoes, beans, bay leaves and stock; stir to combine. Cook, covered, on low setting for 4 hours.
2 Stir in spinach; cook, covered, on high setting for 5 minutes or until spinach wilts. Season to taste.
3 Serve curry topped with paneer and micro herbs.

serving suggestions Serve curry with warmed naan bread, steamed basmati rice, lime wedges or Greek-style yoghurt.

PREP + COOK TIME 1 HOUR SERVES 4

VEGIE DRAWER DHAL *with cheese balls*

This recipe can be made with any vegetables you have in the fridge, especially those looking a bit old. Add 'hard' vegetables such as carrots or potato that require longer cooking, at step 2 and 'soft' vegetables such as peas, towards the end of step 3.

250g (8 ounces) cottage cheese
¾ cup (105g) cornflour (cornstarch)
2¼ teaspoons garam masala
3 cloves garlic, crushed
2 tablespoons vegetable oil
1 medium onion (150g), chopped finely
1 bunch fresh coriander (cilantro) (100g)
2 tablespoons grated fresh ginger
2 fresh long red chillies, chopped finely
2 cups (240g) coarsely chopped vegetables (such as pumpkin, baby eggplant, cauliflower, peas, spinach)
1 cup (200g) dried red lentils
1 litre (4 cups) vegetable stock
2 cups (400g) basmati rice
3 cups (750ml) water
vegetable oil, extra, for deep-frying

1 Combine cottage cheese, ½ cup cornflour, ¼ teaspoon garam masala and 1 garlic clove in a medium bowl. Season. Refrigerate until required.

2 Heat oil in a large saucepan over medium heat; cook onion, stirring, for 5 minutes or until softened. Remove leaves from coriander; reserve. Finely chop coriander stalks and roots, add to pan with ginger, 1 chilli, remaining garam masala and garlic, and any 'hard' vegetables that take longer to cook (such as pumpkin and cauliflower); cook for 2 minutes.

3 Add lentils and stock to pan; bring to the boil. Reduce heat to low; cook, stirring occasionally, for 25 minutes. Add any 'soft' vegetables (such as peas and spinach); cook for a further 5 minutes or until all vegetables are cooked.

4 Meanwhile, place rice and the water in a medium saucepan; bring to the boil. Cover, reduce heat; cook for 15 minutes. Remove pan from heat; stand, covered, for 5 minutes.

5 Fill a large saucepan one-third full with extra oil; heat to 180°C/350°F (or until a cube of bread turns golden in 15 seconds). Using damp hands, roll 2-teaspoonfuls of cheese mixture into balls. Roll in remaining cornflour to coat. Deep-fry balls, in batches, for 1 minute or until light golden and crisp. Drain on paper towel.

6 Top dhal topped cheese balls, remaining chilli and reserved coriander leaves; serve with rice.

TIPS The cheese balls may take on a rustic, slightly 'burst' appearance if left in the oil for too long. This is fine, they will just not look as round. Wash coriander roots well before using. Store dried lentils and rice in the fridge to stop the invasion of pantry moths.

PREP + COOK TIME 1 HOUR SERVES 6

sweet potato & eggplant curry WITH CAVOLO NERO & CURRY LEAVES

Meaning 'black cabbage' in Italian, cavolo nero is more delicate and sweet than its relative curly kale, while possessing many of the same great nutritional qualities; it is rich in protein, fibre, antioxidants, vitamins A, C, and K, and folate.

650g (1¼ pounds) baby eggplants
olive-oil spray
⅓ cup (80ml) olive oil
1 large onion (200g), chopped finely
4cm (1½-inch) piece fresh ginger (20g), chopped finely
1 fresh small red chilli, chopped finely
2 cloves garlic, crushed
4 cardamom pods, crushed lightly
1 teaspoon garam marsala
1 teaspoon ground cumin
1 teaspoon ground turmeric
800g (1½ pounds) orange sweet potato, cut into 3cm (1¼-inch) pieces
270ml canned coconut milk
400g (12½ ounces) canned diced tomatoes
1 cup (250ml) vegetable stock
1 tablespoon brown mustard seeds
24 fresh curry leaves
400g (12½ ounces) cavolo nero (tuscan cabbage), chopped coarsely
2 tablespoons water

1 Preheat oven to 180°C/350°F. Line two oven trays with baking paper.
2 Quarter eggplants lengthways; place on trays, spray with oil. Bake for 20 minutes or until golden and soft.
3 Heat 2 tablespoons of the oil in a large heavy-based saucepan over medium-high heat; cook onion, ginger, chilli and garlic for 3 minutes. Reduce heat to low, add cardamom, garam marsala, cumin and turmeric; cook for 2 minutes. Increase heat to medium, add sweet potato; stir to coat in spices.
4 Add coconut milk to pan with tomatoes and stock; bring to the boil. Reduce heat to low-medium; simmer, covered, for 20 minutes or until sweet potato is tender. Stir in eggplant; return to the boil. Season to taste.
5 Meanwhile, heat remaining oil in a large frying pan over medium-high heat; cook mustard seeds, stirring, for 1 minute or until seeds pop. Add curry leaves; cook for 1 minute. Stir in cavolo nero and the water; cook, covered, until just wilted. Season to taste.
6 Serve curry with cabbage mixture.

serving suggestion Serve with steamed basmati rice and Greek-style yoghurt.

Sauces

SALSA VERDE

PREP + COOK TIME 5 MINUTES MAKES ⅔ CUP

Process or blend 2 cups firmly packed fresh flat-leaf parsley leaves, 1½ tablespoons loosely packed fresh lemon thyme leaves, 1 tablespoon capers, 1 crushed clove garlic, 1 teaspoon caster sugar, ½ cup olive oil and 1½ tablespoons white wine vinegar until combined. Season.

MANGO CHUTNEY YOGHURT

PREP + COOK TIME 5 MINUTES MAKES 1¼ CUPS

Combine 1 cup (280g) Greek-style yoghurt and 2 teaspoons lemon juice in a small bowl; season to taste. Swirl through 2 tablespoons store-bought mango chutney. Season with freshly ground black pepper

RAITA

PREP + COOK TIME 5 MINUTES (+ REFRIGERATION & STANDING) MAKES 1¾ CUPS

Place a fine sieve over a bowl, spoon in 500g (1lb) Greek-style yoghurt and ½ teaspoon salt. Cover, refrigerate 2 hours until thicker; discard liquid. Combine 1 peeled, coarsely grated lebanese cucumber and ½ teaspoon salt; stand 20 minutes. Squeeze out excess liquid. Combine yoghurt, cucumber, 1 clove crushed garlic and 2 tablespoon chopped fresh mint leaves. Season to taste.

HARISSA YOGHURT

PREP + COOK TIME 5 MINUTES MAKES 1 CUPS

Combine 1 cup (280g) Greek-style yoghurt and 1 teaspoon honey in a small bowl; season to taste. Swirl through 2 teaspoons harissa paste; serve sprinkled with ½ teaspoon ground cumin.

PREP + COOK TIME 1 HOUR SERVES 4

Thai yellow CURRY

We used a mix of shiitake, oyster and enoki mushrooms in this recipes, but you can use swiss brown or button instead, if you prefer. Fried asian shallots are available from Asian food stores and some supermarkets.

- 1 tablespoon rice bran oil
- 1 medium red onion (170g), sliced thinly
- ¼ cup (75g) yellow curry paste
- 2 cloves garlic, crushed
- 10cm (4-inch) stalk fresh lemon grass, bruised
- 4 kaffir lime leaves, shredded finely
- 1⅔ cups (410ml) coconut milk
- 1 cup (250ml) water
- 750g (1½ pounds) orange sweet potato, unpeeled, scrubbed, chopped coarsely
- 200g (6½ ounces) green beans, trimmed
- 250g (8 ounces) assorted asian mushrooms (see above)
- 1 tablespoon grated palm sugar
- 1 tablespoon fish sauce (see tip)
- 2 tablespoons lime juice
- 1 fresh long red chilli, seeded, sliced thinly
- ¼ cup (20g) fried asian shallots
- ½ cup fresh thai basil leaves

1 Heat oil in a wok or large heavy-based saucepan over high heat; cook onion, stirring, for 5 minutes or until onion softens. Add curry paste, garlic, lemon grass, and kaffir lime leaves; cook, stirring, for 1 minute or until fragrant.

2 Add coconut milk, the water and sweet potato; bring to the boil. Reduce heat to medium, simmer for 20 minutes or until sweet potato is just tender. Stir in beans and mushrooms; simmer for a further 5 minutes or until vegetables are tender. Stir in sugar, fish sauce and juice; remove and discard lemon grass.

3 Serve curry sprinkled with chilli, shallots and thai basil.

TIP If you are avoiding all animal-derived products, use tamari instead of the fish sauce and be careful to check the curry paste label to ensure it doesn't contain any animal products.

PREP + COOK TIME 1 HOUR 15 MINUTES SERVES 4

eggplant PARMIGIANA

Parmigiana has a special place in Australian cuisine, with veal or chicken parmigiana an ubiquitous entry on the local pub's food menu. This eggplant parmigiana is equally delicious and comforting, with its rich tomato sauce, and luscious melted cheese top.

⅔ cup (160ml) olive oil
1 medium onion (150g), chopped finely
2 cloves garlic, crushed
400g (12½ ounces) canned diced tomatoes
2 cups (560g) tomato passata
¼ teaspoon dried chilli flakes
2 medium eggplants (600g), sliced thickly
¼ cup (35g) plain (all-purpose) flour
⅓ cup fresh basil leaves
200g (6½ ounces) bocconcini, sliced thinly
⅔ cup (50g) finely grated parmesan (see tip)
½ teaspoon sweet paprika

1 Preheat oven to 180°C/350°F.

2 Heat 1 tablespoon of oil in a large frying pan over medium heat; cook onion, stirring, for 5 minutes or until softened. Add garlic; cook, stirring, for 1 minutes or until fragrant. Stir in tomatoes, passata and chilli flakes; season to taste. Transfer mixture to a medium heatproof jug.

3 Toss eggplant in flour to coat; shake away excess. Heat remaining oil in same pan; cook eggplant, in batches, until browned on both sides. Drain on paper towel.

4 Layer half the eggplant in a 18cm x 25cm (7¼-inch x 10-inch) ovenproof dish; season. Top with half the tomato mixture, basil and bocconcini. Repeat layering, finishing with parmesan. Sprinkle with paprika.

5 Bake, covered, for 30 minutes. Uncover, bake for a further 15 minutes or until browned and tender. Serve parmigiana sprinkled with extra basil leaves, if you like.

tip Traditionally parmesan is made with calf rennet. When purchasing check ingredients to see that the cheese is vegetarian, make sure it doesn't contain calf rennet.

serving suggestions Serve with a rocket (arugula) salad and crusty bread or stir through cooked short pasta.

PREP + COOK TIME 30 MINUTES (+ STANDING) SERVES 4

dhal with CHUTNEY YOGHURT

Dhal in India is not only the name for lentils, but also the spicy stew that is prepared with them. The ultimate Indian comfort food, there are thousands of variations on the staple, each family with their own recipe.

1 tablespoon peanut oil
1 large onion (200g), sliced thinly
2cm (¾-inch) piece fresh ginger (10g), grated finely
2 teaspoons brown sugar
⅓ cup (75g) korma curry paste
1 teaspoon ground cumin
1 teaspoon ground turmeric
1 teaspoon sweet paprika
400g (12½ ounces) canned diced tomatoes
250g (8 ounces) cherry tomatoes
1 cup (250ml) coconut milk
1 cup (250ml) water
400g (12½ ounces) canned brown lentils, drained, rinsed
400g (12½ ounces) canned chickpeas (garbanzo beans), drained, rinsed
2 tablespoons coarsely chopped fresh coriander (cilantro) leaves

chutney yoghurt
⅔ cup (190g) Greek-style yoghurt
1 tablespoon mango chutney

1 Heat oil in a large heavy-based saucepan over medium heat; cook onion, ginger and sugar, stirring, until soft. Add curry paste and spices; cook, stirring, until fragrant.
2 Add canned and cherry tomatoes, coconut milk, the water, lentils and chickpeas to pan; bring to the boil. Boil for 10 minutes or until mixture thickens slightly. Remove from heat; stand for 10 minutes.
3 Meanwhile, make chutney yoghurt.
4 Sprinkle dhal with coriander; serve with chutney yoghurt.

chutney yoghurt Combine ingredients in a small bowl.

serving suggestion Serve dhal with warm roti bread or steamed basmati rice.

TIPS You can freeze individual portions of dhal in airtight containers for up to 1 month. Thaw overnight in the fridge; reheat in the microwave. Chutney yoghurt is not suitable to freeze.

PREP + COOK TIME 1 HOUR 20 MINUTES SERVES 4

BEAN, SILVER BEET & TOMATO STEW
with almond crumble

If you are not strictly vegetarian, add 2 slices of rindless bacon (130g) to the recipe. Chop bacon finely and cook, with the onion in step 4, until browned lightly. Continue with recipe as directed. Serve stew with crusty sourdough bread or cooked brown rice.

6 medium roma (plum) tomatoes (360g), halved lengthways
½ cup (80g) natural almonds
2 tablespoons olive oil
2 medium onions (300g), chopped finely
2 cloves garlic, chopped finely
1 pinch saffron threads
½ teaspoon cayenne pepper
400g (12½ ounces) canned diced tomatoes
½ cup (100g) dried French-style green lentils
2 cups (500ml) water
750g (1½ pounds) silver beet (swiss chard), trimmed, leaves chopped
150g (4½ ounces) green beans, trimmed, sliced lengthways
1 tablespoon finely grated lemon rind
½ cup chopped fresh curly parsley leaves
30g (1 ounce) butter

1 Preheat oven to 180°C/350°F. Line an oven tray with baking paper.

2 Place tomato halves, cut-side up, on tray; season generously. Roast for 30 minutes or until softened.

3 Meanwhile, spread almonds on a second oven tray; roast on a separate shelf with tomatoes for 10 minutes or until nuts are lightly browned. Process almonds until coarsely chopped.

4 Heat oil in a large heavy-based saucepan over medium heat. Cook onion, garlic, saffron, and cayenne pepper, stirring, for 5 minutes or until onion is softened. Add canned tomatoes, lentils and the water; simmer, covered, for 20 minutes.

5 Add silver beet in two batches; cook, covered, until first batch is wilted before adding the second batch. Stir well. Add beans and roasted tomatoes; simmer, covered, for a further 5 minutes or until beans are tender. Season to taste.

6 Place almonds, rind and parsley in a small heatproof bowl. Heat butter in a small saucepan over medium heat; cook, stirring, until it begins to brown. Pour over almond mixture; stir to combine.

7 Serve stew sprinkled with almond crumble.

PREP + COOK TIME 45 MINUTES SERVES 4

cheesy smoked BAKED BEANS WITH PUMPKIN

Beans are a great vegetarian dinner option, that are packed with protein and fibre, while also being very kind to your wallet. Jap pumpkins are a very sweet variety of squash, also known as kabocha, with an edible skin, and a short, squat shape.

½ cup (125ml) extra virgin olive oil
1 medium red onion (170g), cut into wedges
350g (11 ounces) jap pumpkin, chopped
1.2kg (2½ pounds) canned four-bean mix, drained, rinsed
400g (12½ ounces) canned chickpeas (garbanzo beans), drained, rinsed
1 chipotle chilli in adobo sauce, chopped finely
¼ cup (50g) adobo sauce from canned chipotle chilli in adobo sauce
1 tablespoon honey
2 tablespoons barbecue sauce
1 teaspoon dijon mustard
700g (1½ pounds) tomato passata
¾ cup (90g) coarsely grated cheddar
⅓ cup (40g) coarsely grated smoked cheddar
2 cloves garlic, crushed
4 x 110g (3½ ounces) ciabatta rolls, halved

1 Preheat oven to 220°C/425°F.

2 Heat 2 tablespoons of oil in a large ovenproof frying pan over high heat; cook onion and pumpkin, stirring occasionally, for 4 minutes or until onion has softened slightly. Add beans, chickpeas, chilli, adobo sauce, honey, barbecue sauce and mustard; cook, stirring occasionally, for 3 minutes or until heated through. Stir in passata; bring to the boil. Boil for 3 minutes or until thickened slightly; season to taste.

3 Sprinkle bean mixture with cheeses. Bake for 15 minutes or until cheese is browned lightly.

4 Meanwhile, combine garlic and remaining oil in a small bowl; season. Brush garlic mixture over cut side of rolls. Place rolls on an oven tray; bake on a separate shelf with beans for 6 minutes or until golden.

5 Serve baked beans with torn garlic bread.

TIPS You can use potatoes or orange sweet potato instead of pumpkin in this recipe if you like. Chipotle chilli with adobo sauce can be found in most good grocers and delicatessens. Recipe is not suitable to freeze.

PREP + COOK TIME 1 HOUR MAKES 4

EGGPLANT & TOMATO STEW
with cheesy yoghurt topping

These little individual cheese-topped stews make the perfect alternative if you are craving a pie, but trying to cut out the pastry (or if you are gluten intolerant!). Eggplant and tomato mixture can be made a day ahead, to the end of step 4.

2 medium eggplants (600g), chopped
1 teaspoon fine sea salt
⅓ cup (80ml) olive oil
1 medium onion (150g), chopped finely
200g (6½ ounces) swiss brown mushrooms, sliced
2 cloves garlic, chopped finely
6 large roma (plum) tomatoes (540g), chopped
⅓ cup coarsely chopped fresh flat-leaf parsley
4 egg yolks
2 eggs
1½ cups (420g) Greek-style yoghurt
1½ cups (120g) finely grated parmesan (see tip)

1 Preheat oven to 200°C/400°F. Place four 2-cup (500ml) shallow ovenproof dishes on an oven tray.
2 Combine eggplant and salt in a colander over a bowl. Stand for 20 minutes.
3 Meanwhile, heat 1 tablespoon of oil in a large frying pan over medium heat. Cook onion, stirring, for 2 minutes or until lightly golden. Add mushrooms; cook, stirring, for 5 minutes or until browned lightly. Add garlic and tomato; simmer for 10 minutes.
4 Pat eggplant dry between sheets of paper towel to remove any excess moisture. Heat half of the remaining oil in a large clean frying pan over high heat; cook half the eggplant, stirring, for 3 minutes or until golden and tender. Repeat with remaining oil and eggplant. Stir eggplant and ¼ cup of the parsley into tomato mixture; season to taste. Spoon eggplant mixture into the dishes.
5 Combine egg yolks, whole eggs, yoghurt and 1⅓ cups of parmesan in a medium bowl. Spoon yoghurt mixture over eggplant mixture in dishes; smooth top. Sprinkle with remaining parmesan. Bake for 12 minutes or until golden. Serve topped with remaining parsley.

tip Traditionally parmesan is made with calf rennet. When purchasing check ingredients to see that the cheese is vegetarian, make sure it doesn't contain calf rennet.

serving suggestion Serve with green leafy salad.

PREP + COOK TIME 5 HOURS 45 MINUTES SERVES 4

LENTIL & CAULIFLOWER STEW

with carrot-top pistou

You will need a slow cooker for this recipe.

¾ cup (150g) French-style green lentils
400g (12½ ounces) baby (dutch) carrots with tops
1 tablespoon olive oil
2 medium leeks (700g), white part only, sliced thinly
3 cloves garlic, crushed
2 stalks celery (300g), trimmed, sliced thickly
4 sprigs fresh thyme
2 dried bay leaves
1 cup (250ml) dry white wine
2 cups (500ml) vegetable stock
½ medium cauliflower (750g), cut into medium florets
2 medium kale leaves (70g), stalks removed, shredded coarsely

carrot-top pistou

1½ cups coarsely chopped reserved carrot tops
1 cup loosely packed fresh mint leaves
2 teaspoons finely grated lemon rind
1 tablespoon lemon juice
1 clove garlic, quartered
½ cup (125ml) olive oil

1 Rinse lentils well; drain.

2 Trim carrots, reserving tops to make pistou.

3 Heat oil in a 4.5-litre (18-cup) slow cooker on sauté (MEDIUM) setting; cook leek and garlic, stirring, for 10 minutes or until lightly browned. Add carrot, celery, thyme and bay leaves; cook, stirring, for 5 minutes or until vegetables soften. Add wine; bring to the boil. Boil, uncovered, for 1 minute.

4 Add stock, cauliflower and lentils; stir to combine. Cook, covered, on low setting for 5 hours, stirring occasionally.

5 Discard thyme and bay leaves. Add kale to cooker; cook, covered, on high setting for 10 minutes or until kale wilts. Season to taste.

6 Meanwhile, make carrot-top pistou.

7 Serve stew topped with pistou.

carrot-top pistou Blend or process reserves carrot tops, mint, rind, juice and garlic until finely chopped. With motor operating, add oil, in a thin, steady stream; process until smooth. Season to taste.

serving suggestion Serve with brown rice or crusty bread to mop up the juices.

PREP + COOK TIME 30 MINUTES SERVES 4

MUSHROOM RAGÙ
with soft polenta

30g (1 ounce) butter
500g (1 pound) cup mushrooms, sliced thickly
3 cloves garlic, crushed
½ cup (125ml) vegetable stock
150g (4½ ounces) soft goat's cheese
¼ cup fresh flat-leaf parsley leaves

soft polenta

2 cups (500ml) milk
2 cups (500ml) vegetable stock
1 cup (170g) instant polenta (cornmeal)
40g (1½ ounces) butter, chopped
¾ cup (60g) finely grated parmesan (see tips)

1 Heat butter in a large heavy-based frying pan over high heat; cook mushrooms, stirring occasionally, for 5 minutes or until mushrooms are browned lightly and most of the liquid is evaporated. Season. Add garlic; cook, stirring, until fragrant. Stir in stock; bring to the boil. Reduce heat to medium; simmer for 2 minutes or until most of the liquid has evaporated. Season to taste; cover to keep warm.

2 Meanwhile, make soft polenta.

3 Pour polenta immediately onto a serving board or plate; using the back of a spoon, make slight indents in polenta. Spoon mushrooms over polenta using a slotted spoon; drizzle with some of the pan juices. Top with small chunks of goat's cheese; sprinkle with parsley.

soft polenta Bring milk and stock to the boil in a large saucepan. Gradually add polenta, stirring constantly. Reduce heat; cook, stirring, for 10 minutes or until polenta thickens. Stir in butter and parmesan. Season to taste.

serving suggestion Serve with a mixed herb salad.

TIPS Traditionally parmesan is made with calf rennet. When purchasing check ingredients to see that the cheese is vegetarian, make sure it doesn't contain calf rennet. You could also serve the polenta topped with ratatouille ormixed roasted vegetables such as pumpkin, onion, capsicum and zucchini.

Glossary

ALLSPICE also called pimento or jamaican pepper; tastes like a combination of nutmeg, cumin, clove and cinnamon. Available whole or ground.

BASIL

sweet the most common type of basil; used extensively in Italian dishes and one of the main ingredients in pesto.

thai also known as horapa; different from holy basil and sweet basil in both look and taste, with smaller leaves and purplish stems. It has a slight aniseed taste and is one of the identifying flavours of Thai food.

BAY LEAVES aromatic leaves from the bay tree available fresh or dried; adds a strong, slightly peppery flavour.

BEANS

black also called turtle beans or black kidney beans; an earthy-flavoured dried bean completely different from the better-known Chinese black beans (fermented soybeans). Used mostly in Mexican and South American cooking.

borlotti also called roman beans or pink beans, can be eaten fresh or dried. Interchangeable with pinto beans due to their similarity in appearance – pale pink or beige with dark red streaks.

butter cans labelled butter beans are, in fact, cannellini beans. Confusingly butter is also another name for lima beans, sold both dried and canned; a large beige bean having a mealy texture and mild taste.

cannellini a small white bean similar in appearance and flavour to other white beans (great northern, navy or haricot), all of which can be substituted for the other. Available dried or canned.

green also known as french or string beans, this long thin fresh bean is consumed in its entirety once cooked.

haricot the haricot bean family includes navy beans and cannellini. All are mild-flavoured white beans which are interchangeable.

kidney medium-size red bean, slightly floury in texture yet sweet in flavour; sold dried or canned, it's found in bean mixes and is used in chilli con carne.

lima large, flat kidney-shaped, beige dried and canned beans. Also known as butter beans.

snake long (about 40cm), thin, round, fresh green beans, Asian in origin, with a taste similar to green or french beans. Used most frequently in stir-fries, they are also known as yard-long beans because of their (pre-metric) length.

white a generic term we use for canned or dried cannellini, haricot, navy or great northern beans belonging to the same family, phaseolus vulgaris.

BUK CHOY also known as bok choy, pak choi, Chinese white cabbage or Chinese chard; has a fresh, mild mustard taste. Its mildly acrid, distinctively appealing taste has made it one of the most commonly used Asian greens.

BUTTER use salted or unsalted (sweet) butter; 125g (4 ounces) is equal to one stick of butter.

BUTTERMILK originally the term given to the slightly sour liquid left after butter was churned from cream, today it is made from no-fat or low-fat milk to which specific bacterial cultures have been added. Despite its name, it is actually low in fat.

CARDAMOM a spice native to India and used extensively in its cuisine; can be purchased in pod, seed or ground form. Has a distinctive aromatic, sweetly rich flavour.

CHEESE

bocconcini walnut-sized, baby mozzarella; a delicate, semi-soft, white cheese traditionally made from buffalo milk. Sold fresh, it spoils rapidly so will only keep, refrigerated in brine, for 1 or 2 days at the most.

cheddar the most common cows' milk 'tasty' cheese; should be aged, hard and have a pronounced bite.

fetta Greek in origin; a crumbly textured goat- or sheep-milk cheese having a sharp, salty taste. Ripened and stored in salted whey; particularly good cubed and tossed into salads.

fetta, persian a soft, creamy fetta marinated in a blend of olive oil, garlic, herbs and spices; available from most major supermarkets.

goat's made from goat milk, has an earthy, strong taste. Available in soft, crumbly and firm textures, in various shapes and sizes, and sometimes rolled in ash or herbs.

parmesan also called parmigiano; is a hard, grainy cow-milk cheese originating in the Parma region of Italy.

provolone a mild stretched-curd cheese similar to mozzarella when young, becoming hard, spicy and grainy the longer it's aged.

CHICKPEAS (GARBANZO BEANS) also called hummus or channa; an irregularly round, sandy-coloured legume used extensively in Mediterranean, Indian and Hispanic cooking. Firm texture even after cooking, a floury mouth-feel and robust nutty flavour; available canned or dried (reconstitute for several hours in cold water before use).

CHILLI use rubber gloves when seeding and chopping fresh chillies as they can burn your skin. We use unseeded chillies because the seeds contain the heat; use fewer chillies rather than seeding the lot.

CHINESE COOKING WINE also called shao hsing or chinese rice wine; made from fermented rice, wheat, sugar and salt with a 13.5% alcohol content. Inexpensive and found in Asian food shops; if you can't find it, replace with mirin or sherry.

CORIANDER (CILANTRO) also called pak chee or chinese parsley; bright-green-leafed herb with a pungent flavour. The leaves, stems and roots of coriander are also used. Also available ground or as seeds; these should not be substituted for fresh coriander as the tastes are completely different.

CREAM, THICKENED (HEAVY) a whipping cream containing thickener. Minimum fat content 35%.

CRÈME FRAÎCHE a mature, naturally fermented cream (minimum fat content 35%) having a velvety texture and slightly tangy, nutty flavour.

FENNEL also called finocchio or anise; a crunchy green vegetable slightly resembling celery that's eaten raw in salads; fried as an accompaniment; or used as an ingredient in soups and sauces. Also the name given to the dried seeds of the plant which have a stronger licorice flavour.

GAI LAN also known as chinese broccoli, gai larn, gai lum and chinese kale; appreciated more for its stems than its coarse leaves.

GALANGAL a rhizome with a hot ginger-citrusy flavour; used similarly to ginger and garlic. Use fresh ginger if unavailable.

GARAM MASALA a blend of spices including cardamom, cinnamon, cloves, coriander, fennel and cumin, roasted and ground together.

KAFFIR LIME LEAVES also known as bai magrood and looks like two glossy dark green leaves joined end to end, forming a rounded hourglass shape. Used fresh or dried in many South-East Asian dishes, they are used like bay leaves or curry leaves, especially in Thai cooking. Sold fresh, dried or frozen, the dried leaves are less potent so double the number if using them as a substitute for fresh; a strip of fresh lime peel may be substituted for each kaffir lime leaf.

LEMON GRASS also known as takrai, serai or serah. A tall, clumping, lemon-smelling and tasting, sharp-edged aromatic tropical grass; the white lower part of the stem is used, finely chopped, in much of the cooking of South-East Asia. Can be found fresh, dried and frozen in supermarkets and Asian food shops.

LENTILS (red, brown, yellow) dried pulses often identified by and named after their colour. Eaten by cultures all over the world, most famously perhaps in the dhals of India, lentils have high food value.

French-style green lentils related to the famous French lentils du puy; these green-blue, tiny lentils have a nutty, earthy flavour and a hardy nature that allows them to be rapidly cooked without disintegrating.

OIL

olive made from ripened olives. Extra virgin and virgin are the first and second press, respectively, of the olives and are therefore considered the best; 'light' refers to taste not fat levels.

peanut pressed from ground peanuts; most commonly used oil in Asian cooking because of its high smoke point (capacity to handle high heat without burning).

vegetable oils sourced from plant rather than animal fats.

ONIONS

green (scallions) also called, incorrectly, shallot; an immature onion picked before the bulb has formed, has a long, bright-green edible stalk.

red also known as spanish, red spanish or bermuda onion; a sweet-flavoured, large, purple-red onion.

SAFFRON stigma of a member of the crocus family, available ground or in strands; imparts a yellow-orange colour to food once infused. The quality can vary greatly; the best is the most expensive spice in the world. Should be stored in the freezer.

SUGAR

caster (superfine) finely granulated table sugar.

brown a soft, finely granulated sugar retaining molasses for its characteristic colour and flavour.

palm also called nam tan pip, jaggery, jawa or gula melaka; made from the sap of the sugar palm tree. Light brown to black in colour and usually sold in rock-hard cakes; use light brown sugar if unavailable.

white (granulated) coarse, granulated table sugar, also known as crystal sugar.

TAMARIND PASTE the distillation of tamarind pulp into a condensed compacted paste with a sweet-sour, slightly astringent taste. Thick and purple-black, it requires no soaking.

YOGHURT, GREEK-STYLE often made from sheep milk that is strained in a cloth (traditionally muslin) to remove the whey and to give it a thick, smooth, creamy consistency.

Conversion chart

MEASURES

One Australian metric measuring cup holds approximately 250ml; one Australian metric tablespoon holds 20ml; one Australian metric teaspoon holds 5ml.

The difference between one country's measuring cups and another's is within a two- or three-teaspoon variance, and will not affect your cooking results. North America, New Zealand and the United Kingdom use a 15ml tablespoon.

All cup and spoon measurements are level. The most accurate way of measuring dry ingredients is to weigh them. When measuring liquids, use a clear glass or plastic jug with the metric markings.

The imperial measurements used in these recipes are approximate only. Measurements for cake pans are approximate only. Using same-shaped cake pans of a similar size should not affect the outcome of your baking. We measure the inside top of the cake pan to determine sizes.

We use large eggs with an average weight of 60g.

DRY MEASURES

METRIC	IMPERIAL
15G	½OZ
30G	1OZ
60G	2OZ
90G	3OZ
125G	4OZ (¼LB)
155G	5OZ
185G	6OZ
220G	7OZ
250G	8OZ (½LB)
280G	9OZ
315G	10OZ
345G	11OZ
375G	12OZ (¾LB)
410G	13OZ
440G	14OZ
470G	15OZ
500G	16OZ (1LB)
750G	24OZ (1½LB)
1KG	32OZ (2LB)

LIQUID MEASURES

METRIC	IMPERIAL
30ML	1 FLUID OZ
60ML	2 FLUID OZ
100ML	3 FLUID OZ
125ML	4 FLUID OZ
150ML	5 FLUID OZ
190ML	6 FLUID OZ
250ML	8 FLUID OZ
300ML	10 FLUID OZ
500ML	16 FLUID OZ
600ML	20 FLUID OZ
1000ML (1 LITRE)	1¾ PINTS

LENGTH MEASURES

METRIC	IMPERIAL
3MM	⅛IN
6MM	¼IN
1CM	½IN
2CM	¾IN
2.5CM	1IN
5CM	2IN
6CM	2½IN
8CM	3IN
10CM	4IN
13CM	5IN
15CM	6IN
18CM	7IN
20CM	8IN
22CM	9IN
25CM	10IN
28CM	11IN
30CM	12IN (1FT)

OVEN TEMPERATURES

The oven temperatures in this book are for conventional ovens; if you have a fan-forced oven, decrease the temperature by 10-20 degrees.

	°C (CELSIUS)	°F (FAHRENHEIT)
VERY SLOW	120	250
SLOW	150	300
MODERATELY SLOW	160	325
MODERATE	180	350
MODERATELY HOT	200	400
HOT	220	425
VERY HOT	240	475

Index